PREFACE

This overview of legal processes related to courts explains—for lawyers, law students, and others interested in law—the relationships among different adjudicative processes and the central structural problems that all procedural systems have to address. A fuller elaboration of the challenges can be found in the book *Adjudication and its Alternatives: An Introduction to Procedure* (Foundation Press, 2003), co-authored with Owen M. Fiss. That book and this volume continue to reflect much that we learned with and from Robert M. Cover, with whom we wrote *Procedure* (Foundation Press, 1988).

*

For Jonathan Curtis–Resnik, within the hopes of a world more fair than this, and for Denny Curtis, who continues to help bring such a world about.

*

ABOUT THE AUTHOR

Judith Resnik is the Arthur Liman Professor of Law at Yale Law School, where she teaches courses on procedure, federal courts, feminist theory, and large-scale litigation. Professor Resnik is a graduate of Bryn Mawr College and New York University School of Law, where she held an Arthur Garfield Hays Fellowship.

She is the co-author (with Owen Fiss) of the book ADJUDICATION AND ITS ALTERNATIVES: AN INTRODUCTION TO PROCEDURE (Foundation Press, 2003). Recent contributions to books include the chapter *Civil Processes* in THE OXFORD HANDBOOK OF LEGAL STUDIES (eds. Peter Cane & Mark Tushnet, Oxford Press, 2003) and *The Rights of Remedies: Collective Accountings for and Insuring Against the Harms of Sexual Harassment*, in DIRECTIONS IN SEXUAL HARASSMENT LAW (eds. Catharine MacKinnon and Reva Siegel, Yale Press, 2003). Professor Resnik's articles include *Trial as Error, Jurisdiction as Injury: Transforming the Meaning of Article III*, 113 Harvard Law Review 924 (2000); and *Managerial Judges*, 96 Harvard Law Review 374 (1982).

Professor Resnik has chaired the Section on Procedure, the Section on Federal Courts, and the Section on Women in Legal Education of the American Association of Law Schools. She has served on committees and task forces of the American Bar Association, is a member of the American Law Institute, and was a consultant to the Institute for Civil Justice of RAND. She is also an occasional litigator and court-appointed expert. In 2001, she was elected a member of American Academy of Arts and Sciences and, in 2002, a member of the American Philosophical Society.

*

TABLE OF CONTENTS

PROCESSES OF THE LAW

UNDERSTANDING COURTS AND THEIR ALTERNATIVES

*

INTRODUCTION

During the twentieth century, the prospect of adjudication became plausible for whole new sets of claimants, both inside the United States and beyond. The reasons are many, but four factors stand out.

First, the state came to be understood as *itself* subject to regulation, as bound by its own rules, as obliged to treat persons with dignity and respect. Individuals gained the right to use litigation to call state officials to account and thereby to hold government to its own promises.

Second, in part through new information technologies, patterns of injuries experienced by large numbers of individuals became visible. The growing appreciation for the scope and patterns of injuries prompted interest in fashioning means to provide remedies to large numbers of similarly situated individuals.

Third, the growth of the profession of lawyers provided the personnel to generate regulations and to staff efforts to challenge various forms of injury. The development of the legal profession is a story unto itself, but the expansion of the legal profession is a predicate to procedural elaboration.

A fourth factor, one that has been under-appreciated in the literature of courts, is women's rights. Women only gained juridical voice in the last century, and the radical reconceptualization of women as rightsholders—both in and outside of their families—has changed the range of disputes now understood as legally viable. Related is the recognition that persons of all colors and economic strata are entitled to participate in and to use law.

As demand has grown for adjudication, governments have responded in part by diversifying the venues for adjudicative decisionmaking. Courts are no longer the only places for adjudication. Administrative agencies and tribunals are now central providers, as are many private systems, stemming from contractual agreements between union and management, between consumer and manufacturer, between university and student. Moreover, as technology altered the import of geographical boundaries, political and commercial exchanges emerged that alter assumptions about the relationship between national boundaries and the jurisdiction of courts. Transnational disputes have become more frequent, and concepts of universal jurisdiction have been elaborated.

Governments have also changed the modes of adjudication to provide more decisionmakers and more flexible forms of decision for the growing queue of claimants. While once judges were identified solely with adjudication, today they are multi-taskers, managing cases and proposing that parties settle their disputes. What most governments have not done is subsidize the processes sufficiently to make either adjudication or its alternatives available across the economic spectrum. Lawyers remain gatekeepers for those seeking to pursue claims, and the lack of legal services impedes access for a range of claimants to a variety of processes.

Further, many are ambivalent about the desirability and utility of heavy reliance on adjudication. While some praise the possibilities of adjudication in recognizing the dignity and rights of persons, others are more critical of such regulatory modes and seek to shift disputants to more private and less combative processes.

The twentieth century is thus filled with examples of the expansion of adjudicatory opportunities and of their contraction. Below, I provide an overview of the current options. While my lens is on adjudication and its alternatives, the debate about these processes is linked to other debates—about the desirability of substantive rules of liability, the role of and the market for lawyers, and political conceptions of the utility and propriety of regulation. In short, understanding the world of procedure requires appreciation for the history of its transformation and proliferation during the twentieth century, for the diversity of its current forms, and for the political currents and social movements prompting both praise and criticism.

Yet despite the many variations and venues, it is also possible to track common themes. All processes need to respond to a core problem: distributing power among claimants and between claimants and third-party decisionmakers. Whether based in public institutions or predicated on private contract, all procedural systems allocate authority and all affect the immediate disputants and third parties. All must also cope with the differential resources of disputants.

In brief, whatever the kind of proceeding, it begins because someone (an individual, a group, the government) brings a claim against another and argues that a legal norm has been violated. Whether brought in a state-based dispute resolution system or in a grievance system created by a private institution such as a corporation or a school, a third party (sometimes called a judge) is called upon to respond. That third party may turn the issue back to the disputants—urging them to solve the problem themselves or offering to serve as an intermediary for settlement. Alternatively, that third party could be authorized—by parties' agreements or by the state—to determine the validity of the claim. That judgment could be advisory or binding and final, either when issued or after review by other decisionmakers.

This book identifies the commonalities as well as the distinctions among adjudication, alternative dispute resolution (ADR), and dispute resolution (DR), among small and large-scale proceedings, and among processes labeled "civil," "criminal," and "administrative." I begin with a simplified linear outline of how cases, both civil and criminal, move through the federal courts. Included is discussion of individual and aggregate case processing as well as of how jurists decide which kinds of claims, raised by which individuals, entities, or groups, can be pursued in court.

I then map the different structures—courts, both domestic and international, agencies, and privately constituted tribunals—in which litigation and its alternatives occur. Thereafter, I describe the participants who are central to these various but interrelated systems, and I pay particular attention to the roles played by jurors, judges, and lawyers. Also explored are the challenges posed by the costs of process, which are imposed upon disputants who differ in their economic capacities and access to other resources. Throughout, I note social science research on the frequency and distribution of disputes and the demography of the participants. A concluding discussion explains how court-based procedural rules are made. The central question there is how to allocate the power to make rules, and I use federal civil rulemaking as illustrative of changing answers over the last one hundred years. As readers will see, some chapters include many references to relevant statutes, rules, and cases, whereas in other chapters, I offer overviews of doctrines developed through case law as well as syntheses of empirical research and of commentary on legal processes.

My hopes are threefold: to map the landscape of processes for responding to disputes, to enable those interested in or concerned about process to participate in contemporary debates about the legitimacy and desirability of reformatting opportunities to challenge authority, and to enlist a wider audience in thinking about the relationship among justice, equality, and process.

I. CIVIL ACTIONS

Individuals and groups often disagree. At some point, outsiders may characterize the discord as a dispute, but only a small percentage of such disputes result in the filing of a civil lawsuit. Although popular imagery suggests the too-frequent filing of lawsuits, slow processing, and many trials, research on dispute resolution reveals that in many instances, individuals "lump it" (as anthropologists of dispute resolution put it), living with a problem rather than leveling blame and making claims.

The costs of pursuing remedies are high—in terms of time, energy, and money. Lawyers serve as gatekeepers, especially to courts, because attorneys are experts in identifying disputes that have both legal merit and a likelihood of success. Lawyers are also gatekeepers for a less attractive reason: their fees make the process of seeking redress prohibitively expensive for many. Indeed, one reason for the development of new procedures in courts and of privatized resolution outside of courts is to reduce the role of lawyers and thereby lower the cost of disputing.

For example, one study estimated that, in disputes involving more than one thousand dollars, claimants filed lawsuits (in either federal or state courts) in about 11 percent of the cases. Once filed, relatively few cases end by trial; in that study, under 8 percent were tried and more than 50 percent concluded through voluntary agreement of the parties. More recent federal court data indicate that, of 100 civil cases filed, a trial is commenced in about three. Do not, however, assume that all the remaining cases are settled. Rather, estimates are that in about 35 percent of federal civil cases, judges decide the merits short of trial, for example by rendering a ruling that a case has no legal merit. In terms of the pace of litigation, given that most cases are resolved without trial, many conclude relatively promptly. As of 2000, the median time in federal courts from filing to disposition of all civil cases was about eight months; when cases were tried, the median time to disposition was 20 months.

When the litigation world is viewed from the baseline of all the potential disputes, the rate of filing is relatively low. In contrast, the numerical volume of disputes is significant, as are the range and scope of dispute resolution systems. State courts in the United States play the largest role. In 2001, for example, in the state courts, some 93 million cases were filed. About 55 million involved traffic violations. Almost 8 million related to family life. Just under 16 million were contract, tort, or real property cases, and another 14 million were criminal cases. These cases were filed in the more than 15,000 state trial courts that are staffed by about 30,000 trial judges, commissioners, and referees.

Turning to the federal system, some 260,000 civil and about 60,000 criminal cases are begun yearly in the 94 federal trial courts, which also receive more than a million bankruptcy petitions annually. Tens of thousands of proceedings are commenced each year before federal administrative adjudicators. Moving on to privately-based dispute resolution processes, no central database currently answers the question of how many individuals use those processes. One organization, the American Arbitration Association, reports that in 2000, it provided arbitrators and mediators for nearly 200,000 proceedings, a number approaching that of the civil docket of the federal courts.

Commentators debate how to assess the volume of cases filed, with disagreement about the import both of the numbers themselves and of the use of litigation. Critics claim "litigiousness," that too many lawsuits are filed and that reliance on lawsuits is an inefficient means of regulation. Others disagree, arguing that numerical volume is a meaningless measure unless understood in relationship to several other variables, including population growth, major social upheavals (such as wars and economic crises), technological innovations (the invention of the car), and changes in available remedies. For example, when women gained the status of rightsholders, new areas of litigation—relating to rights in and outside of families—came into being. In a parallel fashion, when workers' compensation systems were developed in many states, a significant proportion of cases shifted out of court systems. Similarly, when New Zealand adopted a "no fault" system for car accidents, a substantial reduction in filings followed. Moreover, some commentators argue that robust reliance on litigation is a socially and politically appropriate method to enable public and private enforcement of legal norms.

For those who do pursue legal remedies, a series of decisions are required about how to frame a dispute and from whom to seek redress. While some disputants proceed *pro se* (for themselves), the court-based system is geared to lawyers providing representation. In theory, lawyers serve as agents for clients. In practice, lawyers do not always inform clients of the available options and clients often rely on lawyers' expertise and defer to their decisions. Because of the prevalence of decisionmaking short of trial, many lawyers concentrate on fact investigation, drafting motions and briefs, negotiating settlement, discovery, and arguing motions. In large metropolitan areas, such lawyers are often referred to as "litigators" and are distinguished from "trial lawyers" who examine witnesses in courts.

In terms of the initial issues to be decided, a first question is about the options: can disputants pursue claims in court or are they limited to an ADR process? In a growing number of contracts—signed by employees, consumers, and purchasers of services such as health care—resort to courts is prohibited; only permitted is the use of alternative dispute resolution processes. Moreover, those who can use court-based remedies are sometimes required to pursue remedies in sequence, such as going first "to exhaust" administrative remedies before going on to court. In some instances, one tribunal may have exclusive authority, but often state, federal, tribal, foreign, and international courts have overlapping jurisdiction to hear a dispute. That jurisdictional power can be based, in turn, on the subject matter of the dispute as well as on where the parties can be required to appear. Strategic considerations, such as one party's view that a particular forum would be advantageous because of its proximity or familiarity, also influence decisions about what remedies to pursue and in which order.

Below, I provide a contemporary snapshot of federal civil litigation. The early part of that century produced a major procedural reform. As Chapter VII explores in greater detail, in 1938, the Supreme Court promulgated the first-ever set of national civil rules for all kinds of cases. The 1938 rules aimed to be "transsubstantive"—to provide one set of rules no matter the subject matter of the case. That transsubstantive model was, for a few decades, celebrated as a sustainable solution to procedural challenges.

But, while those rules remain in force today and provide an important template, their content has shifted substantially. One source of pressure on the 1938 model comes from a shift in the kinds of cases litigated and the volume of complaints. For example, while some cases proceed with an individual plaintiff and a single defendant, the last sixty years have also seen an increase in aggregate processing, by which groups litigate either as a class or because courts have grouped individually-filed lawsuits together to facilitate processing. Impetus to change rules comes also from the development of new technologies, such as photocopiers and computers, that expand the amount of information available for investigation and exchange. Further, the growth in the size of law firms and the rise of hourly rates generate incentives to exploit certain features of rules, such as increasing the use of discovery.

In response (and undermining to some extent the transsubstantive premise of the 1938 rules) came new rulemaking, as the Federal Rules have themselves been many times amended nationally and supplemented locally. Further, atop the Federal Rules, Congress has enacted statutes that impose special procedural rules for certain types of cases, sometimes characterized by the kind of dispute (i.e. prison reform litigation, securities cases) and sometimes by the number of disputants or value of claims (large-scale or complex cases). In addition, within the Federal Rules are provisions for each district to draft its own "local rules," provided that they are consistent with the nationwide rules. In practice, there are more than 5000 local rules, some at variance with the nationwide rules. Each district judge may also have his or her own rules, called "standing orders." Thus, lawyers must consult not only the Federal Rules of Civil Procedure, but also relevant case law and statutes (both federal and in some cases, state), non-United States law if applicable, a district court's local rules, and a particular judge's personal glosses on the rules. Further, when bankruptcy petitions are filed in federal court, a specific set of statutes and rules govern those proceedings, primarily heard by a special set of federal judges called bankruptcy judges. Competing models for procedural systems are increasingly common, as specific federal statutes may have special procedures for a given right, as many states and non-United States jurisdictions continue their own procedural formats, and as parties to contracts fashion their own mini-procedural systems.

In short, during the later part of the twentieth century, two somewhat conflicting trends emerged. First, dispute resolution processes and institutions proliferated, undermining the centrality of the Federal Rules with their conception of transsubstantive procedure. Second, as transnational exchanges became easier, pressures built for procedural convergence across the globe, with calls for universal jurisdiction and common procedural rules.

Keep the sense of shifting trends and an appreciation of both the volume of cases and gaps in coverage in mind as you turn now to the simplified model of a lawsuit, which is provided below by using the Federal Rules of Civil Procedure. Given the multiplication of procedural systems, the Federal Rules serve as a vehicle for exploring the issues common to procedural systems rather than as constituting the rules that will necessarily dominate a lawyer's own experiences. (Citations are to relevant titles of the United States Code and to Federal Civil, Criminal, and Appellate Rules.)

A. Pursuing a Federal Civil Action

In the federal system, a "civil action" is commenced by the filing of a *complaint* (Fed. R. Civ. P. 3) and the payment of a $150 filing fee unless the litigant can claim indigence and obtain court permission to proceed *in forma pauperis*, as a poor person. 28 U.S.C. § 1915. (In some state courts, a lawsuit is commenced when the defendant is served with the complaint.) A complaint is the document that provides a description of the case and must identify the basis for the court's subject matter jurisdiction, the identity of the parties, the claims for which relief is sought, and the requested relief. Fed. R. Civ. P. 8. Occasionally, more specificity is required. See, e.g., Fed. R. Civ. P. 9. The question of how much information should be included within a complaint is one that has been the source of sustained debate. While many characterize the Federal Rules as requiring "notice" pleading (minimal information to put the defendant "on notice" of the claim), some courts believe that, in certain areas of law, greater specificity must be provided. Some states have what is termed "fact" or "code pleading," requiring a complaint to detail more of the factual bases of the claim.

Once the complaint is filed, the clerk of the court issues a *summons*, which, along with the complaint, must be served upon the named defendants within a specified period of time and in a particular manner that is reasonably calculated to provide the defendant with notice of the pending action. Fed. R. Civ. P. 4. A series of amendments to that rule now facilitate service by mail and respond to the challenges of serving complaints outside the district in which the case is filed and beyond the borders of the United States. Upon receipt of the complaint and the summons (often referred to as the *process*), a defendant has several options. A defendant may do nothing, called a *default,* which risks entry of an adverse judgment. Note that doing nothing may be an efficient response for those defendants who have no defenses on the merits and from whom a sum certain is sought. Fed. R. Civ. P. 55. Alternatively, within a specified amount of time (generally 20 days), a defendant may respond by *motion* or *answer*.

Motions are requests that the court issue an order, such as asking that a complaint be dismissed for any of a variety of reasons, including that the complaint presents no legal claim, the court selected lacks power (jurisdiction) to hear the case or to bind the parties, the defendant has been sued before by the plaintiff and judgment was entered, essential individuals have not been joined in the litigation, or the complaint lacks sufficient specificity, or other defects. See Fed. R. Civ. P. 8, 9, 11, 12, 19. Certain objections (such as to the jurisdiction of the court over the defendant) must be made promptly or they are waived. If a defendant responds by motion, the court must rule on the request. If the defendant's motion is denied, or if a defendant does not file a motion attacking the complaint, then the defendant must, within a specified number of days, answer the allegations in the complaint.

An answer is a response on the merits. The answer repeats the numbers of each of the paragraphs of the complaint and indicates the defendant's admission, denial, or absence of information about each allegation. An answer is often a list of numbered paragraphs, followed by "admit," "deny," or "defendant has no information which enables the defendant to admit or deny the allegation." Answers may claim that the plaintiff has erred about the facts and, as a consequence, is not entitled to relief. In addition to affirming or negating the factual predicates of a complaint, answers may also include *affirmative defenses*: allegations that, given the information added, the plaintiff ought not prevail. See Fed. R. Civ. P. 8(c). Answers may also include *counterclaims* in which the defendant states claims against the plaintiff or requests dismissal of the complaint. Some of a defendant's arguments can be made either by answering or by filing a motion to dismiss; thus, in practice, the line between motions and answers sometimes blurs. For example, by answer or motion, a defendant may claim that parties "indispensable to the litigation" (those who must participate so that the court can resolve the issue) have not been included. Fed. R. Civ. P. 19. A defendant may also file a *cross-claim* against another party on the theory that the party will be liable to the defendant for the judgment that might result. Fed. R. Civ. P. 14. Complaints, answers, counterclaims, and cross-claims constitute *pleadings*; these documents consist of allegations made by the parties. Fed. R. Civ. P. 7. Once a complaint and answer have been filed, the issue (the matter in dispute) has been *joined*.

The plaintiff may also file motions to amend pleadings, to add new claims or parties (Fed. R. Civ. P. 15), or to seek certification of a case as a *class action*. Fed. R. Civ. P. 23. In addition to motions made by the parties named in the complaint, third parties (those named by neither plaintiffs nor defendants as parties to the case) may also request, again by motion, the court's permission to let them *intervene* and thereby to participate in the litigation. Fed. R. Civ. P. 24. Through such motions, parties and sometimes outsiders struggle over the scale of a lawsuit, as they seek to include others or to require group-based processing. Courts may also formally or informally require consolidation of pending cases. See Fed. R. Civ. P. 42 and 28 U.S.C. § 1407.

A variety of other motions may be filed during the pleadings stage of litigation. In addition to a defendant's motion to dismiss the action (one form of which is called, in some jurisdictions, a *demurrer*) and to motions related to the structure of a lawsuit, either party may seek *temporary restraining orders* or *preliminary injunctive relief* (Fed. R. Civ. P. 65), asking for immediate court assistance on the grounds that one party is in danger of being irreparably damaged, is likely to win on the merits, and is in need of protection during the pendency of the action. A temporary restraining order may, in rare instances, be issued without notice to the other party; the petitioner must, however, explain the reason for the failure to notify the opponent. A temporary restraining order is limited to a ten day period, subject to one renewal or an agreement for an extension. In contrast, a preliminary injunction, which can only be entered after notice and a hearing, may be in effect for the duration of the case. For preliminary injunctive relief, courts generally receive evidence, often in the form of documents but sometimes by holding hearings at which witnesses testify. Such hearings are usually more abbreviated than trials on the merits; the underlying theory of a preliminary injunction is that relief is needed before a full trial can be held. In some cases, however, the hearing on a preliminary injunction is consolidated with the trial on the merits; witnesses testify and are cross-examined, and documents are submitted to the court.

Other motions can also be used to resolve disputes. For example, either party may seek *judgment on the pleadings* (Fed. R. Civ. P. 12) or may request *summary judgment* (Fed. R. Civ. P. 56), asking that the court conclude the case because no material facts are in dispute and, as a matter of law, one party is victorious. Judgments on the pleadings are based solely on information before the court by virtue of the pleadings, while, when considering summary judgment motions, courts may look beyond the pleadings to affidavits or to information obtained by discovery. Therefore, motions for summary judgment are usually accompanied by *affidavits* or what some jurisdictions call *declarations*—written statements of fact that are sworn to by the individual having personal knowledge of the factual statements made. If the opponent claims that facts have been misstated, she or he will need to submit affidavits providing a different version of the events, and sworn to by a person with personal knowledge of the events.

The motions referred to in the Federal Rules are not an exclusive list; parties may need help or seek court relief on other matters not specifically mentioned by the rules. Since a motion is simply a request to the court for an order, parties draft motions and invent the appropriate titles—such as motions for disqualification of counsel, for extensions of time, for reconsideration of an earlier decision, for permission to have a lawyer who is not admitted within a given jurisdiction come before the court ("pro hac vice," translated as "for this occasion") to appear in a specific case.

One of the innovations of the creation of national rules of civil procedure in the 1930s was the provision for a *pre-trial*, a meeting between lawyers and judges to discuss a case before trial. During the twentieth century, the pre-trial conference developed from a voluntary meeting to a mandatory session at which a scheduling order is shaped that provides for the timing of motions, for the parties to exchange information through discovery, and for discussion of settlement. Fed. R. Civ. P. 16. That rule now provides for conferences to occur (by phone, video conference, or in person) within 120 days of the filing of a civil complaint. Thereafter, the judge enters an order outlining the issues agreed upon and the projected schedule, and this order controls the litigation but can be modified "to prevent manifest injustice."

The expansion and development of the Rule 16 process involves a shift in role for federal trial judges, who over the course of sixty years have moved from a posture licensing a good deal of party autonomy to a more managerial stance, and from a focus on adjudication to one supportive of settlements. Whether such a change is wise is a subject of debate. The evolution of that judicial role has been enabled by an administrative decision by most federal district courts to adopt an individual calendar system (in which judges are assigned specific cases from filing to conclusion) as contrasted with a master calendar system (in which different judges work on phases of the same case). District judges sometimes assign both pre-trial management and discovery supervision to magistrate judges, who are judicial officers appointed by the district court for renewable terms of eight years, and who function sometimes as assistants and increasingly as additional judges. See 28 U.S.C. §§ 631 et seq.

Pre-trial conferences provide one of many occasions on which judges can discuss settlement. When initially created in 1938, the pre-trial rule did not address settlement, but in revisions in the 1980s and 1990s, settlement became an express topic of the pre-trial process. Settlement is promoted in part because of the costs and time required by litigation and in part because of a view that agreed-upon outcomes are preferable to adjudicated ones. These settlement efforts are supported by formal sanctions as well as informal practices. For example, if a defendant files a written offer of settlement, the plaintiff is at risk of having to pay costs if the plaintiff declines the offer but then wins less at trial than was offered in settlement. Fed. R. Civ. P. 68. Judges may also encourage settlement by requesting or requiring that litigants submit disputes to specific alternative dispute resolution processes, such as "court-annexed" arbitration or mediation programs.

The 1938 Federal Rules of Civil Procedure also created *discovery*, a process by which parties investigate cases and exchange information under the umbrella of court rules. As with other aspects of the pre-trial process, the rules have been amended many times, with changes sometimes in the direction of additional litigant autonomy but more recently focused on increasing judicial control. For example, in the 1970s, judicial superintendence relaxed as parties were licensed to seek documents from each other without first obtaining court permission. See Fed. R. Civ. P. 34, as amended. In contrast, in response to perceptions of insufficient voluntary exchanges, withholding of information, abusive requests, and overuse, other amendments have increased judicial oversight, authorizing monetary and other sanctions as detailed in Rules 26 and 37.

Major innovations in the 1990s both supplemented the discovery system with obligations of *disclosure* (first provided on a voluntary basis, as districts could by local rule "opt out," and now required nationally) and with limitations on the scope and quantity of discovery. Under the system that had been in place from the 1930s to the mid 1990s, parties were obliged to respond to discovery requests for information about the "subject matter" of disputes, a fairly wide charter that enabled, through Federal Rules 26 through 37 and 45, demands for information from other disputants and sometimes from third parties. In 2000, the grounds for discovery were narrowed; inquiry is available only for materials that support claims or defenses in contention (rather than the "subject matter" in general). Further, amendments place presumptive caps on the quantity of questions and the duration of questioning, and the rules authorize judges to weigh the value of information production against its costs. See Fed. R. Civ. P. 26(a)(b). The new rules made discovery easier in one respect: they require that each side volunteer certain details to the other about persons and materials that can substantiate "disputed facts alleged with particularity in the pleadings." See Fed. R. Civ. P. 26(a). In general, discovery rules require parties to confer and to devise an overall discovery plan; their decisions come under judicial supervision through the Rule 16 conference.

In terms of techniques, the discovery rules permit parties to obtain written information by *interrogatories* (questions), to take *depositions* (in which witnesses are examined by lawyers outside the presence of a judge or jury), to receive documents (by *requests for production*), to inspect property, and to have physicians examine opponents when physical or mental conditions are in dispute. While a great deal of information must be provided, exceptions are made for privileged matters (for example, attorney-client or doctor-patient information) and lawyers' *work product* (materials created by attorneys in preparation for trial). Further, not all methods of discovery are available when dealing with non-parties; for example, interrogatories may only be served upon parties to a lawsuit. Fed. R. Civ. P. 33.

Parties and their witnesses are obliged to comply with discovery requests. If either side is recalcitrant, the opponent can, by motion, request court aid. Motions to *compel* discovery seek court orders to require responses to discovery. See Fed. R. Civ. P. 37. If a party is uncooperative and puts on the opponent the burden of seeking such orders, the court may sanction that party by assessing attorneys' fees and other costs of having to litigate issues relating to the request for information. In addition, courts may impose the penalties of limiting the use of information at trial or precluding litigation on certain issues. Parties may also seek court aid in sheltering them from discovery. Motions for *protective orders* ask courts to permit the party against whom discovery is sought not to reply—for example on the grounds that the questions involve privileged matters or are too burdensome. See Fed. R. Civ. P. 26(c).

Discovery has a variety of strategic uses, some more honorable than others: to obtain data, to assess the likelihood of success and the propriety of settlement, to prepare for trial, to impose costs on the opponent, to expose weaknesses in an opponent's position. Because of the potential costs of information and the value of the data sometimes uncovered (such as the history of one party's failure to remedy a known dangerous condition), discovery is a central feature of civil litigation. Discovery is thus the centerpiece of a debate about the utility of information and its overabundance and about the difficulties of calibrating attorneys' incentives to obtain necessary information but not to engage in wasteful or aggressive forays.

Turn now to the trial process, which is numerically unlikely but which dominates popular perceptions of courts. As noted, fewer than 3 percent of federal civil cases (totaling some 6,500 trials) were tried by federal district court judges in 2001; more than half were *bench trials*, tried to a judge, and the remaining were jury trials, with juries ranging in size from six to twelve individuals. A comparable number of criminal trials took place (as is discussed in Chapter II). The jury system (also discussed in Chapter VI) is a feature of the United States Constitution. The Seventh Amendment preserved the right to a jury trial if available in "suits at common law." Under English practice, the King's courts provided common law remedies, whereas the Chancellor resolved "equitable" disputes. In today's federal courts, litigants have a right to jury trial if their cases would have been tried by juries under the common law system of the late eighteenth century. When the matter would not have been tried by a jury—such as a request for an injunction—judges decide the matter. The Seventh Amendment has been interpreted to apply only to federal courts; state court jury rights may be broader.

Having the right to a trial by jury does not automatically result in a jury trial; to exercise the right requires a specific request for a jury. Fed. R. Civ. P. 38. If litigants waive their right to a jury trial, or if the relief requested is equitable, a judge decides the case. Fed. R. Civ. P. 39. If a jury trial is requested, then jurors are selected by a process called the *voir dire*, during which the judge (and sometimes, in state courts, the lawyers) asks questions of prospective jurors about their ability to decide the case fairly. Fed. R. Civ. P. 47. Each party may challenge jurors for *cause,* a claim that information about a person raises questions of her or his ability to be impartial. In addition, each side is given a specified number of *peremptory* challenges, permitting the discharge of potential jurors without any explanation. Civil juries can include no fewer than six and no more than twelve people. Absent party stipulation, a unanimous verdict is required. Fed. R. Civ. P. 48. In most civil actions, whether tried by judge or jury, the party asserting a fact is required to prove the fact by a preponderance of the evidence.

The Federal Rules of Evidence govern how parties present information to courts. Once witnesses and documentary evidence have been provided, the parties may renew motions to end the case in whole or part by requesting a *judgment as a matter of law* (replacing what was called a *directed verdict*), arguing that a judge ought to enter judgment on the grounds that "no legally sufficient evidentiary basis [exists] for a reasonable jury to find for that party on that issue." See Fed. R. Civ. P. 50(a). If the request is rejected, the lawyers make closing arguments and, after previewing proposed instructions with the parties, the judge instructs the jury about the governing legal rules. Counsel for both parties may ask the judge to give special instructions on relevant issues and may object to the judge's charge to the jury. Fed. R. Civ. P. 51. After hearing the instructions, the jury retires to deliberate in secret and to return a verdict. The jury need not give any reasons for its verdict; typically, the jury returns a *general verdict* (for example, that the defendant is liable). Occasionally, a judge asks a jury to render *special verdicts* or to answer interrogatories, a series of questions posed to clarify the factual predicates to decisions. Fed. R. Civ. P. 49.

In bench trials, the district judge to whom the case has been assigned will, in general, try that case. Upon parties' consent, magistrate judges may also preside at civil trials. See Fed. R. Civ. P. 73 and 28 U.S.C. § 636(c). Unlike the selection of juries, the parties have no right to seek another judge for trial. While a few states permit peremptory challenges of judges, the federal system does not. On rare occasions, a judge may voluntarily *recuse* him or herself or the parties may so request, on grounds described in 28 U.S.C. §§ 144 and 455, such as that the judge has personal knowledge or connections to a dispute. In bench trials, the presiding judge may have a more relaxed attitude towards evidentiary restrictions, perceiving that a court can evaluate information "for what it is worth" given legal constraints. When judges render verdicts, however, they are required— unlike juries—to provide "findings of fact" and "conclusions of law." Fed. R. Civ. P. 52. Further, in cases involving complex relief, ranging from school desegregation litigation to mass torts, the parties may participate in the drafting of the judgment or decree, which can include the creation of auxiliary institutions such as monitors, masters, committees, and claims facilities to assist in the implementation of the decree. See Fed. R. Civ. P. 53.

Once a verdict has been returned, a party may renew its motion for *judgment as a matter of law* (the term now also used after trial in lieu of a motion for "judgment notwithstanding the verdict," or the earlier, Latin, non obstante verdicto, judgment n.o.v.) or may seek a new trial. See Fed. R. Civ. P. 50 and 59. If a judge denies the motion, the judge will enter the verdict as a judgment. See Fed. R. Civ. P. 54 and 58. Thereafter, a party can seek to have the judgment amended (within ten days, under Fed. R. Civ. P. 59) or, under very limited circumstances, vacated because of clerical errors, in light of new evidence, or for other specified reasons. Fed. R. Civ. P. 60.

The entry of judgment does not always end the dispute at the trial level. If the losing party fails to comply with the court order, the winner must return to court to seek enforcement of the judgment. When money is at issue, the winner seeks *execution* on the judgment. Federal courts rely on state practices to order assets seized and, if necessary, auctioned to fund delinquent payments. Fed. R. Civ. P. 69. Further, if individuals violate court orders, the sanction of contempt is available in two forms. In what is termed *criminal contempt*, courts impose fines or imprisonment as punishment for the violation of their orders. In contrast, *civil contempt* is predicated upon ongoing noncompliance. Fines and imprisonment end when the order is obeyed because civil contempt is designed to force the recalcitrant party to comply with the order. See 18 U.S.C. § 401 and Fed. R. Crim. P. 42.

B. Appellate Review

Once judgment has been entered, the aggrieved litigant may appeal to a federal intermediate appellate court. 28 U.S.C. §§ 1291 and 1292. Generally, under the *final judgment rule*, litigants have a right to appeal only after the entry of final judgment. Some state systems permit more appeals at earlier stages. A party does so by filing a *notice of appeal* with the trial court within a specified time period; failure to file in a timely fashion can constitute a waiver of the right to appeal. See Rules 3 and 4 of the Federal Rules of Appellate Procedure (Fed. R. App. P.), supplemented by each federal circuit's own local rules. A few appeals—such as those contesting the grant or denial of preliminary injunctive relief and those involving issues that cannot be effectively reviewed at the conclusion of the case—can be taken *interlocutorily*, during the pendency of the case. In addition, district judges may certify that an issue is so central to the disposition that it merits interlocutory review and, if the appellate court agrees, appeal can be had prior to the end of the lawsuit. 28 U.S.C. § 1292(b). More recently, special rules have been added to provide for discretionary review of class action orders. See Fed. R. Civ. P. 23(f).

Remember that from the time before a lawsuit is filed and through its appeals, parties can continue to negotiate. Thus, appeals can be filed as a means of prompting a settlement for less than was awarded at the trial level. Further, and parallel to developments at the trial level, staff attorneys work to screen cases, and appellate courts have developed settlement programs, in which their staff meet with lawyers to urge that parties negotiate a solution in lieu of an appellate decision. Fed. R. App. P. 33. Note also that the filing of a notice of an appeal does not *stay* the judgment. Rather, judgments become effective upon their entry unless an appellant succeeds in convincing either the district or appellate court to grant a stay, that is, an order suspending the execution of the judgment. Fed. R. App. P. 18. The standard for stays is like that for preliminary injunctions. The question is the likelihood of success on the merits and whether irreparable harm will occur if the judgment is effective prior to plenary review.

If settlement does not occur, appellate judges rule on the basis of excerpts of the record below and written briefs. Fed. R. App. P. 28, 30. Occasionally, one or more *amicus curiae* ("friend of the court") may seek to file briefs in support of one side. Fed. R. App. P. 29. Not all federal appellate courts provide parties with rights to argue orally, and when oral arguments are permitted, the time allotted may be as short as ten minutes per side. Fed. R. App. P. 34. Panels of three judges make most of the decisions; rarely are their decisions reconsidered, either by that panel or *en banc*. Fed. R. App. P. 35.

Appellate courts typically take one of three approaches to rulings rendered below. Consideration of issues of law are *de novo*, meaning that appellate courts make the decision afresh, with no special deference to the trial court's view of the legal issues. In contrast, trial judges' factual findings can only be set aside only if "clearly erroneous." Fed. R. Civ. P. 52. Somewhere in between stands the "abuse of discretion" standard, which accords some deference to the trial court's judgment. Appellate courts may affirm in whole or part or reverse and remand, generally to the judge who erred below but, on unusual occasions, to a judge other than the one who tried the case initially.

The losing party at the appellate stage may seek review by the United States Supreme Court. Litigants may in rare circumstances attempt to invoke the Court's so-called mandatory appellate jurisdiction; virtually all proceed instead by requesting discretionary review through filing petitions for a writ of certiorari. See 28 U.S.C. §§ 1253, 1254, 1257–59, and Supreme Court Rules 10–16. The Court chooses to hear very few cases, selected either because of conflicting rulings in the circuits or because of the importance of a legal issue. Oral arguments in the Supreme Court generally permit each side one half hour; special permission is needed for more than one attorney per side to participate. Sup. Ct. R. 28. A rich understanding of the Court's procedures can be gained by reading Robert L. Stern, Eugene Gressman, Stephen M. Shapiro, & Kenneth S. Geller, Supreme Court Practice (8th ed. 2002).

A word on the volume of cases as they go through the system is in order. At the trial level, some 260,000 civil cases are filed in federal courts yearly. As noted, of 100 cases filed, fewer than three reach trial and of those tried, roughly half are tried by a judge and half by a jury. About 60,000 criminal defendants are charged annually, and trials begin in about six cases out of 100. Many state courts have similarly low trial rates for contract and tort cases.

At the appellate level, the courts of appeals receive about 55,000 appeals yearly. In 2000, they rendered decisions in 27,000 cases. Of those decisions, about 22,000 were "not published." While available to the litigants on databases, decisions designated by courts as "not for citation" cannot be invoked as precedent by other litigants when arguing their cases. Recent controversy over this practice has reduced its use somewhat, and prompted proposals to change rules to enable litigants to cite all relevant prior decisions. Given the appellate courts' ability to select which cases get full briefing, argument, and decision, some commentators believe that while technically a "right of appeal" remains for all civil litigants, in practice, a triage system has developed with many cases receiving cursory review.

Turning to the Supreme Court, in 2000, it received more than 7,000 requests to hear cases. More than two-thirds of those were *pro se*, by litigants who were not represented by lawyers. In contrast to the large number of requests, the Supreme Court decided less than 100 cases that year. The number of written decisions has declined in recent years from about 115 in 1992 to about 80 in 2000.

C. Claims for Relief and Aggregate Processing

Recounted thus far is the process by which civil cases move through court-based processes from filing to disposition. In each, an individual or entity identifies a particular harm that law recognized to be a legal right. Such plaintiffs had a *cause of action* (or, in the terms of the Federal Rules of Civil Procedure, a *claim for relief*) that if substantiated, entitles them to a remedy.

What kinds of injury do courts recognize as requiring their response. What number of persons can seek remedies in the same proceeding and through what format? Responses to these questions fill case law reporters and legal commentary. Here a much abbreviated overview is presented to enable readers to understand the changing composition of court-users and of cognizable claims.

In the United States, individuals, entities, associations, corporations, the government, and even groups specially constituted for the purpose of pursuing a particular legal right may all bring claims to courts. But what claims are eligible for court review and which will be rejected as outside a court's purview? Within the federal system, answers are framed by reference to the United States Constitution, which in Article III gives federal courts jurisdiction over *cases* and *controversies* but which defines neither term. State systems may also speak of "cases" but because Article III does not directly govern state court processes, those jurisdictions are free to define the requisite elements of a case differently than do the federal courts.

What might the word "case" entail? Under current (and much debated) doctrine of the United States Supreme Court, plaintiffs must show that because of some form of "injury in fact," they have a "personal stake" that has been affected by a defendant's behavior and that can be redressed through an order issued by a court. In many instances, this showing can readily be made. And, in many areas, such as torts, family law, and contracts, in which disputes involve private actors, the question is discussed by asking whether a plaintiff has a "cause of action" against a defendant.

Where do causes of action come from? Causes of action stem from common law rights, statutes, and occasionally state or federal constitutions. Deciding which forms of injury merit legal protection can be difficult and the answers have changed over time. For example, the common law once recognized the tortious alienation of affections, but most jurisdictions no longer do. New causes of action also come into being, either through common law and constitutional development or by legislation. Illustrative are the Married Women's Property Acts, which states enacted during the nineteenth century to overturn common law rules that married women had no right to bring claims in their own names and to hold contract and property rights independent of their husbands.

Judicial interpretation is required to create or to abolish causes of action based on the common law. But many statutes straightforwardly create causes of action by providing that persons injured may bring lawsuits to enforce rights. Sometimes, such as in the example of employment discrimination, statutes require individuals to bring claims first to administrative agencies for resolution; litigation can only occur after efforts are first made to obtain redress elsewhere. Often, however, plaintiffs may go directly to court.

Statutory causes of action may also raise questions requiring judicial interpretation. For example, statutes may create rights (such as to disclosure of information when stocks are offered for sale) and specify that a particular governmental entity (such as the Securities and Exchange Commission) can pursue wrongdoers. But such statutes may not specify whether private parties are also able to pursue claims under their provisions. Hence, proceduralists speak of whether a cause of action is express or whether it can be *implied* from either statutes, regulations, or the Constitution itself and, if so, whether courts should permit damages and injunctive relief.

How should a court decide whether a statute can be the basis for a lawsuit when Congress has said nothing about the role private citizens may play in enforcement of such rights? Should the answer vary depending on whether a plaintiff seeks injunctive or monetary relief? The Supreme Court and lower courts have faced these issues on numerous occasions. In Cort v. Ash, 422 U.S. 66 (1975), the Court set forth a four-part test: Did Congress intend to create a private cause of action? Does the legislative history provide any insight? Would private enforcement be inconsistent with the statutory scheme authorizing a public official to bring suits? Would implication of a private claim provide federal jurisdiction over issues traditionally committed to the states? Under Cort v. Ash, courts were relatively willing to take congressional silence on private causes of action, coupled with congressional silence on the exclusivity of public enforcement, to infer private causes of action to enforce statutory rights.

Beginning in the mid–1980s, however, in split decisions, a majority of the Supreme Court pulled away from liberal implication of private causes of action under either statutes or the Constitution. In terms of statutes, the Court narrowed its focus to the text and then created a presumption that congressional silence on the availability of private causes of action indicated their non-existence. For example, in a case involving the federal statute on the privacy of student records, the Supreme Court held that, because the statute contains no specific provision authorizing private causes of action, it does not create any individually enforceable rights. See Gonzaga University v. Doe, 536 U.S. 273 (2002).

Notice the relationship between the question of causes of action and jurisdiction. If causes of action exist under federal law, jurisdiction is available by virtue of 28 U.S.C. § 1331 (providing federal courts with authority to hear cases that "arise under" federal law), and the volume of cases eligible for filing in the federal courts rises. In contrast, if no private claims can be brought, the level of enforcement of statutory rights will depend entirely upon the federal officials charged with such enforcement. Notice also the interaction between the courts and Congress. If courts hold that a statute does not create a cause of action, Congress has the opportunity—sometimes taken—to amend legislation to so provide. Remember, however, that congressional rightsmaking can be cabined by constitutional provisions, including interpretations of Article III's case or controversy requirement.

Other parts of the Constitution can also be read to affect congressional authority to create rights. For example, the Supreme Court has held (generally 5–4) that the Eleventh Amendment limits the power of Congress to create private rights of action for damages against states, whether pursued in federal or state court. See Board of Trustees of the University of Alabama v. Garrett, 531 U.S. 356 (2001), Alden v. Maine, 527 U.S. 706 (1999).

Other issues include what range of defendants may be held liable, what remedies are provided, and what standards of proof must be met. For example, while the Court has held that Title IX of the Education Amendments of 1972, 20 U.S.C. § 1681(a) (prohibiting a student from being "excluded from participation in, be[ing] denied the benefits of, or be[ing] subjected to discrimination in any education program or activity receiving Federal financial assistance") provides a cause of action for children alleging sexual harassment by teachers, school districts can only be found liable when "the district itself intentionally acted in clear violation of Title IX by remaining deliberately indifferent to acts of teacher-student harassment of which it had actual knowledge." Further, "in the context of student-on-student harassment, damages are available only where the behavior is so severe, pervasive, and objectively offensive that it denies its victims the equal access to education that Title IX is designed to protect." See Davis v. Monroe County Board of Education, 526 U.S. 629, 641, 652 (1999); Gebser v. Lago Vista Independent School District, 524 U.S. 274 (1998).

Turn from these questions of statutory interpretation to constitutional interpretation. Constitutions include many statements of rights but also may not specify mechanisms for implementation. In many instances, the question is avoided because legislatures have created specific litigating rights built on constitutional guarantees. Illustrative is 42 U.S.C. § 1983, enacted after the Civil War and authorizing individuals subjected to deprivations of federal rights by state actors to bring claims in federal court. But what if no statutory remedy is provided? For example, Section 1983 claims run against those acting under state but not under federal law. And what if a statute provides a remedy but a broader one might be implied through constitutional interpretation? Davis v. Passman, 442 U.S. 228 (1979), held that a woman, invoking the Constitution, could bring a lawsuit against a congressman, alleged to have discriminated against her in employment because she was a woman. In an opinion by Justice William Brennan, the Court concluded that it should presume a justiciable controversy in the absence of other mechanisms by which to enforce rights. Because Congress had exempted itself from the federal statute (Title VII) that created rights of action against other employers, the Court held that an implied cause of action directly from the Constitution was appropriate. Since the 1980s, however, the Court's majority has employed a more restrictive approach, and has declined in several instances to infer constitutional protections. See, e.g., Bush v. Lucas, 462 U.S. 367 (1983); Correctional Services Corp. v. Malesko, 534 U.S. 61 (2001).

In addition to disagreements about when to imply causes of action, the debate about what litigants can bring which disputes to court is discussed sometimes by using the term *standing*. Over the course of the twentieth century, as litigants pressed for governments to obey their own laws, the United States Supreme Court started to use the word standing to analyze whether a particular individual or entity could enforce laws limiting governmental authority. For many, the terms "standing" and "cause of action" represent the same concept: is this person entitled to be heard on the merits of whether this defendant breached a legal duty? Further, by equating the two, commentators underscore that a decision concluding that a particular person lacks standing to pursue a claim is, in essence, a judgment on the merits that the person has no legally enforceable right.

Nonetheless, the term standing is now commonplace in public law litigation, with the Supreme Court rendering dozens of rulings on what kind of harm is required for a plaintiff to seek court review. For example, in Sierra Club v. Morton, 405 U.S. 727 (1972), the Supreme Court concluded that the Sierra Club could challenge the Secretary of the Interior alleged to have exceeded statutory powers when authorizing commercial development of a National Park but only if the Sierra Club and its members used that park. The Court recognized that harms to recreational and aesthetic interests, like harms to property or persons, could be the basis of legal action. However, ruled the Court over dissents, were the Sierra Club to allege only a general concern about the environment (as contrasted to a specific allegation of the disruption of personal use), it could not command judicial attention, for it lacked a personal stake—the "injury in fact"—required to pursue the action.

From this approach, questions emerged about what constitutes injury and what organs of government—the courts, the legislatures or the executive—can delineate rights as flowing to individuals. What if the harms were widely shared? More or less abstract? Examples litigated have included disputes about the meaning of constitutional provisions, such as whether the First Amendment prevented the federal government from giving away federal land or buildings to religious organizations and about whether, under the constitutional obligation of the federal government to regularly account for its spending, the Central Intelligence Agency (CIA) had to make disclosures of its expenditures. Similarly, questions emerged under statutes, such as whether the Clean Air Act's provisions that "any citizen" could bring a claim, permitted only those with certain kinds of personal stakes to proceed or whether Congress could authorize a general right of citizens to bring suits to enforce federal laws. Thus far, the Supreme Court has continued to insist on being able to distinguish proper plaintiffs from members of the general public on some grounds and thereby rejecting certain kinds of cases—including the examples involving the Establishment Clause and the CIA accounting. Yet the Court has also concluded that simply because an injury is widely-shared (such as violations of voting regulations) does not preclude plaintiffs from seeking relief.

Moving beyond the federal courts, many jurisdictions—both within and outside the United States—have a conception of standing different than that of current federal law. Illustrative is State ex rel. Ohio Academy of Trial Lawyers v. Sheward, 715 N.E.2d 1062 (Ohio 1999), in which, in a 4–3 decision, the Ohio Supreme Court held "tort reform" legislation (including limitations on monetary damages and altered statutes of limitations) violative of the state's constitutional rules on separation of powers. The lawsuit challenging the legislation had been filed by a trial lawyers' association, which alleged specific harms (through loss of dues, clients, and fees) as well as a more generalized injury. The Ohio Court rejected the concept of "lawyer standing" as too broad but held that injunctive relief could be available without a showing that a plaintiff had "any legal or special individual interest in the result" save being "an Ohio citizen and, as such, interested in the execution of the laws of this state." The court elaborated: "[w]here a public right, as distinguished from a purely private right, is involved, a citizen need not show any special interest therein." The majority called its "public-rights doctrine" an exception to the general personal-injury requirements, and specified that it should only be used "in the rare and extraordinary case" that, comparable to the case at bar, "directly divest[s] the courts of judicial power."

Outside the United States, many countries recognize citizen suits to challenge executive or administrative actions. For example, any "member of the public or social action group acting bona fide" can apply on behalf of a class or individual unable to do so to seek review of administrative action in the Indian courts, which also provide for appointment of commissioners to enhance factfinding resources. Under Canadian law, citizens may also challenge administrative actions upon a showing of no alternative method to bring a case to the courts and a genuine interest in the validity of the action challenged. Under Israeli law, the current approach recognizes *actio popularis*, permitting those without a personal stake to bring actions related to the public interest based on constitutional or other rule-of-law principles.

One potential source of confusion, and a helpful introduction to the discussion of aggregation, is the question of how the idea of causes of action and standing applies to groups or associations. The *Sierra Club* case, discussed above, is illustrative of the fact that entities (including associations, corporations, unions, and the government) can bring lawsuits as individual plaintiffs, seeking relief for themselves. A distinctive question is the capacity of organizations to bring a lawsuit on behalf of their members, and the Supreme Court has on several occasions considered the propriety of groups litigating claims in which their members have interests. A powerful illustration comes from the 1960s, when the State of Alabama sought to obtain membership records of the NAACP in an effort to discourage participation in that group's civil rights efforts. The Supreme Court held that the NAACP could bring the case on behalf of its members who, had they filed directly, would have lost the very privacy they were seeking to protect. See NAACP v. Alabama ex rel. Patterson, 357 U.S. 449 (1958).

By the 1970s, the Court formalized its test of organizational standing to bring suits on behalf of its members. Hunt v. Washington State Apple Advertising Comm'n, 432 U.S. 333, 343 (1977), provides the principles currently operating. In 2000, the "Hunt test" was summarized, in Friends of the Earth v. Laidlaw Environmental Services, 528 U.S. 167, 181 (2000) as follows:

> An association has standing to bring suit on behalf of its members when its members would otherwise have standing to sue in their own right, the interests at stake are germane to the organization's purpose, and neither the claim asserted nor the relief requested requires the participation of individual members in the lawsuit.

Yet another question relates to the idea of many individuals, each with his or her own cause of action, coming together in one lawsuit to act as a group. Many techniques are available within the federal system to enable *aggregation*. For this discussion, I use the term aggregation to include instances when more than one person is litigating, when pre-existing entities are litigating, or when individual cases are grouped with others for some purpose or at some times but not necessarily throughout their life spans.

Below, I first provide an overview of the techniques, both formally established through rules or statutes and informally created by specific judges or lawyers that permit aggregation. Thereafter, I discuss some of the ideas behind aggregate processing. The key point is that, over the last few decades, a profound change has occurred in practice and in attitude toward group litigation. While once aggregation was an exotic event requiring special justification, the presumption has shifted towards acceptance of aggregation as an essential and appropriate response.

A highly visible method for aggregation is the *class action*, available under federal law through Rule 23 of the Federal Rules of Civil Procedure and in many state systems as well. Rule 23 was a product of the 1960s. The Rule was specifically drafted to enable individuals otherwise without access to lawyers and otherwise without remedy to make their way into court.

In the class action, a person steps forward to represent him or herself and others "similarly situated" to redress a legal harm that has injured all within the class specified. As conceived in the 1960s, the named individual must show that he or she is one of a group too numerous to proceed, practically, with each person separately named. Some within that group may not even know that a harm has occurred, while others may not be known to the named representative. The members of the class must each have their own legal right but must also have in common questions of law and fact. Named representatives must be typical of those they seek to represent, have no conflicts of interest with class members, and have the resources and lawyering capacity to provide adequate representation. Further, the party seeking certification of a class action must show either that, if successful in part, inconsistent verdicts would do harm to plaintiffs or defendants or, alternatively, that a class would provide a superior tool for processing the dispute. For example, if a defendant has an insurance policy that provides only one million dollars in coverage but the alleged injuries exceed that amount, the disposition of one plaintiff's lawsuit could impede the ability of other potential plaintiffs to recover. Or, if plaintiffs seek an injunction—desegregating a school—as a practicable matter, that remedy may require the defendant to treat a group of people in a similar fashion.

For many years, courts thought this model inappropriate to tort litigation, conceived as raising questions of individual harm. Further, under rules of choice of law, federal courts had to use state law in many such cases. Were a group constituted, the application of differing legal rules would limit the utility of group processing. But attitudes shifted as cases involving asbestos and medical devices provided examples of tortious injuries shared by thousands of people. While once the typical class action complaints alleged violations of securities laws, other consumer harms, or civil rights claims, today's class actions involve property and personal damage as well. As the use of class actions has grown and radically augmented the resources available to attorneys for plaintiffs, opposition to class actions has also grown, with arguments that some cases provide more to lawyers obtaining large attorney fee awards than to the litigants allegedly harmed. During the 1990s, Congress enacted special statutes to regulate class actions in securities litigation and to prohibit legal service lawyers paid by federal funds from bringing class actions.

While the class action rule (Rule 23) is a much-discussed mechanism in the Federal Rules of Civil Procedure for aggregation, it is not the only way under the Federal Rules for cases to be aggregated. A second technique is *consolidation*. Rule 42 of the Federal Rules authorizes a court to order a joint hearing or trial of any or all the matters in issue in actions "involving a common question of law or fact." Yet a third rule-based technique is *interpleader*, in which a would-be defendant files as a plaintiff and joins persons who have claims against the initiator, who hopes to avoid exposure to "double or multiple liability." *Joinder* is a fourth technique by which multiple parties (and claims) can be brought together. A fifth mechanism is when outsiders *intervene* in an ongoing lawsuit. A sixth, less obvious, rule-based device that might also be characterized as a quasi-informal mechanism for aggregation is Rule 53, which provides for the appointment of special masters or experts. This rule has been used (in asbestos litigation and other cases) to enable a special master to work on a set of cases not officially combined but handled simultaneously.

Federal statutes can enable aggregate litigation in a variety of ways. Statutes can authorize class-like actions when creating specific causes of action or can authorize procedures for group processing of cases invoking a range of legal rights. In addition, Congress can empower either private individuals or government officials to bring lawsuits on behalf of others.

For example, federal statutes can provide both causes of action and authority for groups to pursue claims. One illustration is the Age Discrimination in Employment Act ("ADEA"), under which employees who allege that they have been discriminated against may sue on behalf of themselves "and other employees similarly situated." According to Supreme Court interpretation, that statute gives federal trial courts discretion to facilitate the provision of notice of a pending lawsuit to potential plaintiffs, and such court involvement is appropriate to implement the statutory goals of "avoiding a multiplicity of duplicative suits and setting cutoff dates to expedite disposition of the action." 29 U.S.C. § 621 et seq.

Two important federal statutes that provide procedural mechanisms for aggregate litigation that can involve an array of legal claims are interpleader and bankruptcy. In both, individuals or entities that could have been defendants in lawsuits may come forward as plaintiffs (in the sense of initiators) to commence proceedings in which they admit liability to some people for some amounts, not yet specified. A federal statute, with minimal diversity requirements (in addition to the federal rule described above that relies upon ordinary jurisdictional requirements), provides for interpleader. Federal bankruptcy law is another form of interpleader. The bankrupt is able to pull almost all would-be creditors into one lawsuit. Bankruptcy law provides for an "automatic stay" of previously filed actions. Thus, in contrast to class actions, in which federal courts can generally not stay or otherwise interfere with state court cases, bankruptcy is a more powerful tool—for it can collect virtually all of the claims against the bankrupt in one forum.

The efficacy of bankruptcy as a mechanism of unification is exemplified by the Dalkon Shield litigation, in which, prior to the bankruptcy, two other efforts to aggregate had failed. In the early 1980s, a federal trial court certified a class action but was reversed by the Ninth Circuit. In addition, some cases were transferred for pretrial coordination under the multidistrict litigation statute (discussed below) but then were returned to individual districts. In contrast, via the bankruptcy proceedings initiated in 1985, the manufacturer of the Dalkon Shield was able to draw all filed claims into a single court and then to encourage other potential claimants to file as well. Fewer than 30,000 cases had been filed individually through the tort system before bankruptcy. More than 200,000 claims were received thereafter due to the notification process.

Another statute of great importance in group litigation these days is Section 1407 of Title 28—the provision for multidistrict litigation, or "MDL." This technique grew out of the federal judiciary's concern about "similar" and "protracted" cases filed in district courts across the country. In 1951, the Committee to Study Procedure in Anti–Trust and Other Protracted Cases reported that a "protracted case" "might threaten the judicial process itself," and urged trial judges [to] take control of such cases. After more than a decade of efforts at coordination among judges, the Judicial Conference of the United States requested legislation to authorize transfer and consolidation of cases. In 1968, Congress responded with the multidistrict litigation statute, which authorized a single judge to preside, during the pretrial phase, in the mandatory consolidation of cases pending in federal courts throughout the country.

MDL is thus a statutorily-based (rather than rule-based) mechanism for consolidation of lawsuits. MDL is a possibility when "civil actions involving one or more common questions of fact are pending in different districts." The other statutory criteria are that the transfer must be "for the convenience of the parties and witnesses" and must "promote the just and efficient conduct of such actions." Obviously, these criteria enable many categories of cases to be subject to MDL treatment, and MDL records indicate that cases that have been consolidated pursuant to Section 1407 include antitrust, air disasters, contracts, product liability, copyright and patents, employment, and trademark.

Either by motion of the court or of the parties, cases that are candidates for consolidation are sent to "the panel" on MDL. That panel consists of seven circuit and district judges appointed by the Chief Justice of the United States. The panel decides either to authorize the cases for MDL treatment and to designate a judge to handle them or to decline to permit MDL treatment. No direct appeal of that decision is possible. Under the statute, "review of any order of the panel" is available only "by extraordinary writ" pursuant to the provisions of the All Writs Act, and "[t]here shall be no appeal or review of an order of the panel denying a motion to transfer for consolidated or coordinated proceedings."

After cases have been transferred, subsequently filed cases (called "tag-along actions" that involve "common questions of fact" with cases already transferred) can also be sent to the designated transferee judge. The MDL statute also authorizes the panel to promulgate rules "not inconsistent with Acts of Congress and the Federal Rules of Civil Procedure," and thereby permits nationwide federal procedural rulemaking outside the Rules Enabling Act process.

Under Section 1407, cases in any federal district court can be transferred but are only consolidated "pretrial," for decision of issues such as summary judgment, discovery, and the like. Cases are supposed to be "remanded" to the originating courts at the conclusion of the "pretrial proceedings" for trial, but many cases are disposed of by the transferee judge during the "pretrial" process.

Aggregate litigation also occurs when statutes authorize a government official to pursue litigation on behalf of a group. A myriad of federal statutes create such opportunities. For example, the Civil Rights of Institutionalized Persons Act of 1980 authorizes the Attorney General of the United States to sue states on behalf of institutionalized individuals, allegedly harmed by "egregious" or "flagrant" conditions in state facilities that violate constitutional rights. The Parens Patriae amendments to the antitrust laws enable states to sue on behalf of consumers injured by alleged antitrust violations. The Labor Management Reporting and Disclosure Act gives the Secretary of Labor the power to sue unions that violate obligations of fair election procedures. Sometimes the federal government (or agencies of it) has exclusive authority to litigate; sometimes individuals may litigate concurrently or subsequently. The allocation of authority for rights enforcement between public and private actors was the subject of the debate that helped shape the 1966 amendments to the class action rule and continues to influence current conversations. Aggregation that relies upon the government as a representative is similar to class action aggregation; the political judgments are readily perceived, and the popularity of such activity fluctuates with visions of the appropriate role for government and courts in regulatory activities.

Turn now to more informal methods of aggregation. Doctrine relating both to the process by which cases are decided and to rules on the merits can create aggregation. For example, rulings on *collateral estoppel* and *res judicata* can function in a given series of cases to make a prior ruling apply to subsequent decisions or to abort further decision-making. Legal rules, such as *law of the case* and *stare decisis*, may also create aggregation, either simultaneously or sequentially. Further, expansive or narrow construction of joinder rules and of jurisdictional doctrines such as ancillary and pendent jurisdiction (often called supplemental jurisdiction) can affect aggregative capacities. Finally, liability rules such as enterprise or proportional liability can also produce aggregation.

Moreover, many courts have devised ways to process a group of cases simultaneously—without class certification, rule-based joinder of parties or claims, or MDL designation. The linchpin here is centralization via assignment to a single judge. Sometimes a judge is assigned all cases that involve a particular event or a specific defendant. One vehicle for discovery of the "relatedness" of new cases to those already pending is the federal civil cover sheet, a form that must accompany the filing of all civil complaints. The person who files a complaint is required to state whether the case being filed is "related" to any pending cases. Once such a statement of relatedness is provided, courts often assign the newly-filed case to the same judge assigned to the "related" case. Once judges have a set of cases, whether officially designated "related" or not, judges may order joint discovery, joint pretrial conferences or other forms of standardized, shared proceedings, as well as assign cases to magistrates or special masters for pretrial work. Further, informal cooperation between judges may enable joint processing of cases officially in different jurisdictions, such as those pending in state and federal courts.

Yet another mechanism, often but not always generated as the result of litigation and with the involvement of a judge, is the creation of a "facility" that processes claims and that in many ways is akin to a case-specific agency. For example, for a period of time, a group of asbestos defendants agreed to join in a kind of alternative dispute resolution plan, called the Asbestos Claims Facility. After the demise of that collective, the Manville Settlement Trust was created to process claims against Manville. In the Dalkon Shield case, the trial judge approved the creation of a claims facility to provide payments to claimants, and a variety of procedures, including settlement and arbitration, were developed to process the claims.

Moving from judge-based mechanisms to attorney decisionmaking, lawyers can collect cases in a variety of ways. With court agreement, lawyers can denominate one complaint as a *master complaint,* file cases individually for many people, and have each complaint incorporate by reference the "master" complaint. Alternatively (and to avoid the costs of filing and the accumulation of multiple "cases"), judges may permit the inclusion of many plaintiffs on a single complaint. While not technically a class, the cases may be dealt with by the court as a joint action, with a single set of rulings governing all proceedings.

Aggregation can also occur without a judge working simultaneously on a set of cases; lawyers can have a "stable" or "warehouse" of plaintiff-clients, or represent a defendant sued by many plaintiffs. While in theory and in form each case is separate, in practice lawyers on both sides deal with the cases as a group, sometimes making "block settlements"—in which defendants give a lawyer representing a group of plaintiffs money that is then allocated among a set of clients. Defense lawyers may also pool resources and coordinate activities ranging from raising common defenses to lobbying Congress for legislative change.

Knowledge about these informal mechanisms often comes from direct participants, from social scientists, and from the internet. A variety of communication techniques have evolved—newsletters that keep individual attorneys abreast of case developments, shared discovery, shared experts, and "schools" for training lawyers to try cases of a particular genre. In addition, lawyer-based or lawyer-related institutions, such as the Center for Auto Safety and other consumer monitoring groups, may work in conjunction with lawyers to help them identify injuries, find experts, and work with (or against) regulatory agencies.

Both the informal and formal mechanisms have spawned a set of guidelines or rules, the Manual for Complex Litigation (with its many editions to capture a rapidly-changing landscape), which is an effort to encourage judges to use similar rules in aggregate litigation while tailoring those rules to the particular kind of case presented. But even these guidelines do not capture the breadth of activity and innovation. In the world of aggregation, the rules (to the extent that term is apt) are found in the files of particular cases and in the minds of judges, special masters, magistrates, and lawyers, who formulate procedures as a litigation evolves.

Move from the many different ways in which parties and claims can be aggregated to the larger question of what these many methods represent: a shift from the paradigm of a case between two individuals to a presumption that injuries are often experienced by many people and that remedies need to take into account that wider impact.

Class actions were expressly aimed at enabling litigation—or, to use the words of one of Rules 23's drafters, "even at the expense of increasing litigation, to provide means of vindicating the rights of groups of people who individually would be without effective strength to bring their opponents to court at all." In contrast, the MDL statute was set forth as a vehicle only to expedite litigation already filed. The statute, designed with pending cases in mind, was not cast as a reform to enable those "without effective strength" to litigate but rather as a "management" tool. Unlike class actions, MDL did not become identified as enabling plaintiffs (such as consumers, school children, or prisoners) to file lawsuits otherwise beyond their resources and information. While affecting the outcomes of cases and shifting power among lawyers, clients, and judges, MDL retained its expediting aura. As such, it has been a "sleeper"—having enormous effect on the world of contemporary litigation but attracting relatively few critical comments.

Further, the two functions of aggregate litigation—enabling and expediting—are sufficiently intertwined that one begets interest in the other. If one cannot bring all relevant parties into court, then one cannot end the dispute that embraces them all. Class actions thus become attractive vehicles for some defendants and some judges as means of achieving "global peace" or at least a resolution that would settle a rash of claims. And, for multi-district litigation to do the same required finding ways not just to group cases already filed but also to enable all relevant potential litigants to come into court, again so as to achieve a solution that would have as broad a reach as possible. Thus, some plaintiffs' attorneys, some defendants, and some judges share incentives to process and to settle claims in the aggregate.

As discussed further in Chapters VI and VII, aggregation can significantly alter the resources available to plaintiffs and their lawyers. Through attorneys' fee award rules, plaintiffs and their lawyers have gained resources to engage in forms of lawyering—such as working with media and lobbying—once available only to well-financed defendants. But aggregate litigation also poses challenges for an adjudication system that assumes an identity of interest between litigant and lawyer and that relies on lawyers to represent those interests as faithful agents.

Many questions emerge. How can one structure groups to ensure communality of interest, adequacy of representation, and mechanisms for decisionmaking while litigation is ongoing? Ought members of a class know about pending actions and have any control over the course of its pursuit? Who, for example, ought to have the power to settle such lawsuits? Ought plaintiffs' lawyers make the decisions? With what form of oversight by a court or other third parties?

Such problems of group cohesion exist in all forms of aggregation, whether seeking injunctions (such as to desegregate schools or to alleviate overcrowding in prisons) or damages (such as for injuries for overcharging for services or for exposure to toxic products), whenever the interests of any individual member varies from that of another. Members of groups may have different degrees of injury and different views on priorities among remedies. When the economic stakes are large, another concern emerges: that lawyers representing an aggregate may have more money at stake than any individual claimant—raising questions about how to align incentives to ensure loyal fiduciary agents.

A half century of experience with aggregate litigation has thus not stemmed the debate about its propriety nor ended the challenges entailed in creating groups whose representatives are sufficiently loyal and bonded to those whom them claim to represent. But transformations in technology continue to produce both widespread harms and shared knowledge of injury, making it unlikely that demands for forms of aggregation will abate.

II. CRIMINAL ACTIONS

A. Entering the System

Criminal actions are those initiated by federal, state, or local governments seeking to punish individuals or entities for wrongdoing. The commission of a criminal act does not result in a prosecution unless the fact of an alleged crime becomes known to the government, and governmental authorities exercise their discretion to commence prosecution. The commission of crimes comes to the attention of governments through reporting by victims and by investigation into certain activities.

Just as not all civil disputes result in filings, not all individuals who are victims complain. One study indicated that fewer than half of the incidents eligible were reported to the police. Reporting varies with the type of offense committed; estimates are that victims report more than three quarters of all motor vehicle thefts but only one-half of all burglaries and less than one-third of other thefts. If individuals report criminal activity but the government declines to prosecute, victims who can identify alleged wrongdoers who are not judgment-proof may decide to file civil lawsuits. Although civil remedies may be available, in the United States victims cannot generally compel the government to prosecute.

Even when reports are made, prosecution may not follow. As in civil cases, many factors influence the decision to bring a lawsuit. The prosecution must consider the cost of litigating, the likelihood of success, and the relationship between a specific case and the overall goals of a prosecutor's office. For example, in 2000, the United States government commenced some 63,000 criminal cases in the federal courts, of which about 80 percent were felony prosecutions. Data from state courts indicate about 14 million criminal cases filed there. Volume is not equally distributed; for example, in the federal system, increased interest in enforcing prohibitions on immigration in the 1990s resulted in a concentration of criminal filings in courts along the Southern border. In both state and federal systems, concerns have been raised that certain communities are policed more intensely and that some receive less than their fair share of police protection.

In terms of enforcement personnel, the bulk of the work is done by police officers within state jurisdictions. Federal officials—the Federal Bureau of Investigation (FBI) and other federal agencies including the Drug Enforcement Agency (DEA) and the Internal Revenue Service (IRS)—work only on allegations of criminal activity falling within federal jurisdiction, such as tax violations, securities fraud, bank robberies, and interstate or international criminal activities like mail fraud, narcotics distribution, or terrorism. Cross-designations involve prosecutors or agents from one system working within another; joint task forces use law enforcement personnel from more than one jurisdiction to coordinate efforts for a particular kind of crime. Typical methods of investigation include interviewing witnesses and suspects ("targets" of investigations), collecting information about the alleged crimes, surveillance by electronic devices, and searching suspects' homes, places of employment, and cars for evidence of criminal activity. Investigation may precede arrests, although arrests often occur prior to the completion of an investigation.

The United States Constitution imposes limits on the government's power to investigate crimes. For example, the Fourth Amendment's prohibition on unreasonable searches and seizures has been interpreted to require that police have *probable cause* before they conduct a search. In many circumstances, police must first obtain a *search warrant* providing court permission to search. However, not all searches require a warrant, and some searches may be conducted on less than probable cause. A warrant is not required to search for evidence in "plain view" or when "exigent circumstances" exist. Moreover, police may conduct a brief stop of a person or an automobile when they have some reason to suspect that a law is being violated, even though the level of suspicion is less than "probable cause."

In the federal system, a law-enforcement agent seeking a search warrant must first obtain the approval of an Assistant United States Attorney, who together with the agent submits the warrant application to a federal magistrate judge. The judge then determines if probable cause has been established and if the items being sought are stated with reasonable particularity. Fed. R. Crim. P. 41. The Supreme Court has generally required that both state and federal courts must exclude any evidence in the government's case-in-chief that was obtained in violation of the Fourth Amendment.

At the behest of the prosecution (the United States Attorney for a given district), courts convene *grand juries*. A grand jury is a body made up of sixteen to twenty-three members of the public who hear testimony and receive documents. The grand jury has subpoena power and can command persons to appear and to provide testimony or documents. In practice, prosecutors decide whom to subpoena and what documents to present, using the information to request that a grand jury *return an indictment* against the target of the investigation. Fed. R. Crim. P. 6. The potential defendant has no right to be present at the grand jury. In the federal system, none of the witnesses (including the potential defendant, if called) have the right to have a lawyer with them inside the grand jury room, nor does the potential defendant necessarily have an opportunity to present information to the grand jury in an effort to dissuade it from returning an indictment.

If twelve or more grand jurors concur, an indictment is returned before a judge or magistrate, sitting in open court. Grand jury proceedings themselves are supposed to be kept secret. A court reporter is present to record all the proceedings, which are then sealed. While witnesses may discuss grand jury proceedings, the jurors themselves, as well as prosecutors and government agents, are sworn to secrecy about what occurred. Under specified conditions, information can be released for investigatory purposes and to the defendant. See Fed. R. Crim. P. 6. Grand juries serve until discharged by the court, generally for no longer than eighteen months unless a six-month extension is given because of "the public interest." Fed. R. Crim. P. 6(g).

B. From Prosecution through Conviction

In the federal system, the return of an indictment commences the prosecution of crimes called *felonies*, punishable by more than one year in prison. In some cases, such as those charging only *misdemeanors* and those in which the defendant has waived rights to indictment, the government may instead commence its prosecution by the filing of an *information*, which does not require grand jury action. The indictment is supposed to be a "plain, concise, and definite written statement of the essential facts consisting of the offense charged." Fed. R. Crim. P. 7.

The concept of providing fair notice to defendants of the alleged wrongdoings is central whenever a lawsuit is initiated; in the criminal context, specificity beyond what is currently required on the civil side is demanded. For example, Federal Rules of Criminal Procedure 7(c)(1) mandates that the government name the statutes allegedly violated by the defendant and state the elements of the crimes charged. Indictments or informations, like complaints, may allege more than one offense. The joinder of offenses is limited by a rule that each offense charged be listed in a separate *count* or charge and that, when multiple offenses are joined together, the offenses be of "the same or similar character" or be "based upon the same act or transaction . . . or transactions." Fed. R. Crim. P. 8(a). (In civil actions, although the rules do not require it, complaints often segregate legal claims by separate counts, causes of action, or claims for relief.) Errors or inadequacies in indictments or informations are grounds for dismissal only when they mislead to a defendant's prejudice ("detriment to legal claims"); the documents are construed in favor of validity. Further, while Federal Rules of Criminal Procedure 7(c) requires specificity of the statute or regulation allegedly violated by the defendant, the functional view of sufficiency adopted by courts means that errors in citation are grounds for dismissal only if prejudice can be established.

Because indictments are the product of a grand jury and defendants are entitled to be tried only on facts submitted to a grand jury, indictments may not be amended except by return to a grand jury. However, variances between the facts alleged in the indictment and those proved at trial are allowed, unless defendants can show the loss of substantial rights to be informed of the charges, to be tried on facts submitted to a grand jury, or to plead double jeopardy. In criminal cases, two or more defendants may be joined in the same case as long as they participated in the same act, transaction, or series of transactions. Fed. R. Crim. P. 8(b).

In criminal and civil actions, the commencement of a lawsuit consists of two elements. One is the filing by the initiating party of the appropriate documents with a court. The second is provision of notice to the defendant. On the civil side, notice is typically provided by the service of the summons and complaint, and the defendant responds by filing documents with the court. See Fed. R. Civ. P. 4. On the criminal side, notice usually includes an order that the defendant personally appear, either voluntarily or by arrest. Fed. R. Crim. P. 4.

An individual may be arrested before issuance of either an information or indictment. Although an *arrest warrant* is not constitutionally required in most circumstances, law enforcement agents generally seek warrants to facilitate the process of locating and arresting individuals. In the federal system, the prosecutor secures an arrest warrant by preparing a criminal *complaint* (a "written statement of the essential facts constituting the offense charged"). Fed. R. Crim. P. 3. The complaint includes a brief description of the offense and an affidavit stating the basis for "probable cause." These are sworn to by a complainant (usually a victim or an investigating officer) who appears with the prosecutor before the magistrate judge or district court judge from whom the warrant is sought.

If the complaint and affidavit establish probable cause that the defendant has committed the offense charged, the presiding judicial officer issues a warrant for the arrest. Fed. R. Crim. P. 4, 18 U.S.C. § 3041. If a person is arrested without a warrant having previously been issued, the prosecutor must prepare a complaint and affidavit, which must be sworn to by the complainant, just as is required for arrest warrants. Fed. R. Crim. P. 5(a). If the court determines that insufficient basis (no "probable cause") existed for the arrest, then the defendant is released. In misdemeanor cases, the complaint may serve as the charging instrument throughout the process, although in practice an information is usually filed subsequently. In felony cases, the complaint is only an initiating document; the case cannot go forward until and unless an indictment or information is issued.

The civil analogue of arrest is the seizure of property at issue in a lawsuit—such as freezing funds held in a bank or taking control of real property. Like arrest and detention, seizure may occur before or after permission is requested from a judicial officer. If seizure occurs first, judicial scrutiny must follow within a relatively short time. Similarly, on the criminal side, if police arrest an individual, judicial oversight is supposed to follow promptly to ensure probable cause that the person has committed a crime. When defendants are brought before judicial officials, the initial encounter is called a *presentment* (if no information or indictment has been filed) or an *arraignment* (if following an information or indictment). The federal rules require the presentation of a defendant without unnecessary delay. Fed. R. Crim. P. 5.

If arrested on the basis of a complaint or information rather than an indictment, a defendant has the right to have a preliminary examination (often called a *preliminary hearing*) held within several days of the filing of charges to establish probable cause to *bind over* a defendant to answer; if probable cause is not established, the defendant is *discharged.* This hearing occurs in addition to the presentment. In some states, a preliminary hearing is required even after an indictment has been returned.

The hearing is intended to provide benefits similar to those associated with the grand jury—to buffer the citizenry from decisionmaking by the prosecution and to oblige the government to explain its desire for prosecution to an independent third party, in this instance, the court. In the federal system, magistrate judges are authorized to conduct preliminary hearings. However, the Federal Rules of Criminal Procedure provide that if, prior to the preliminary hearing, a grand jury returns an indictment against the defendant, no preliminary hearing is held. Fed. R. Crim. P. 5. Preliminary hearings are infrequent in the federal system because, once defendants are arrested, prosecutors go to sitting grand juries to obtain indictments. In such cases, defendants are arraigned; when they appear in open court, the charging documents are read to them. Defendants must then respond by *pleading* to the charges. Fed. R. Crim. P. 10. The choices are to plead "not guilty," "guilty," or "nolo contendere" (no contest), which means that a defendant does not admit guilt but does not contest the entry of judgment against him or her.

During these initial meetings with judicial officers, defendants must be informed about how to request *bail* and of their right to counsel. Fed. R. Crim. P. 5. Current federal law requires that the defendant be detained if the government demonstrates that, were the defendant released, the defendant might flee or pose a danger to witnesses or other persons. For example, if the crime charged involved violence, then dangerousness may be established under legal presumptions and bail denied. See Bail Reform Act of 1984, 18 U.S.C. § 3142. Further, under 18 U.S.C. § 3142(e), the statute creates a rebuttable presumption of flight whenever a defendant is charged with certain crimes, including narcotics offenses with sentences of ten years or more. However, a defendant in the federal system may not be detained simply because the defendant cannot raise bail money.

Cases then proceed to resolution, either by dismissal of charges, guilty pleas, or trial. In 2001, trials were completed in about 6 percent of the criminal cases. About 7,000 trials occurred. Some 85 percent of the cases ended in guilty pleas, with acquittal or dismissal of the charges occurring in about 9 percent of the cases. (In the state system, about 6 percent of criminal felony convictions were achieved by trials in 1998). In a few cases, generally in which potential defendants have substantial resources, defendants may be aware of criminal investigations before charges are formally made. Their attorneys may succeed in negotiating settlements pre-indictment, sometimes in exchange for admitting liability civilly or making restitution. Unlike civil actions, which the parties may sometimes dismiss or settle without court approval, criminal charges, once filed, can only be dismissed with permission of the court. Fed. R. Crim. P. 48. However, courts accord prosecutorial decisions great discretion. District court refusals to dismiss charges are rare, in part because of the inability to insist that a recalcitrant prosecutor pursue a given defendant, in part because of awareness that the government may have reasons for dropping one defendant and focusing on others, and in part out of concern for separation of powers.

Most defendants do not have substantial financial resources; lawyering for them begins after they are charged with crimes. The United States Constitution has been interpreted to require the provision of lawyers to indigent defendants if they face the penalty of incarceration. The federal government provides such defense services by one of two means: either paying for attorneys to serve full time as *public defenders* or paying for lawyers (sometimes known as *panel attorneys*), who are selected from a roster, appointed for a particular case, and paid pursuant to the Criminal Justice Act, 18 U.S.C. § 3006A. Such attorneys often have high case loads and limited funds. Panel attorneys are paid on a schedule, often with caps, constraining their resources for investigation and preparation. Thus, pretrial preparation may be minimal. To the extent the prosecution's incentive to negotiate is motivated by fear of adversarial victory, the absence of an intensive defense may result in offers of deals that lack terms favorable to the defendants. One element of a bargain that may inspire the prosecution's interest is defendant cooperation to aid in the investigation of other wrongdoing. Defendants may cooperate ("flip" or "turn") and become prosecution witnesses, undercover informants, or may provide background data on criminal activities. In exchange, charges may be reduced or dismissed.

In the bulk of the cases, negotiations occur between prosecution and defense after the charges have been brought and the pleas made. In some states, judges are involved in *plea bargaining*, but in the federal system, while judges discuss settlement of civil cases, they may not directly join in bargaining in criminal cases. Fed. R. Crim. P. 11(e)(1). Therefore, federal prosecutors cannot make binding promises about what sentences judges will impose. However, by deciding what crimes to charge, prosecutors have the power to set the range of penalties. For example, if a defendant is named in a two-count indictment, the first count may be one in which a maximum term of one year imprisonment and a five thousand dollar fine are allowed, while the second count may be one for which a five year term and a twenty-five thousand dollar fine are authorized by statute. By agreeing to drop a second count, a prosecutor thereby limits a defendant's exposure. A prosecutor can also threaten a defendant that, unless a bargain is made, the defendant will be charged with additional crimes. In bargaining, a prosecutor can also offer to make no recommendation at sentencing or to request leniency.

Further, prosecutorial powers are enhanced when a jurisdiction has—as does the federal system—a sentencing system with either statutory mandatory minimum penalties for certain offenses or binding sentencing guidelines that determine the kinds of sentences to be imposed in light of specific characteristics of a defendant and an offense. Understanding the structure of sentencing is central to understanding the incentives that affect settlement. Provisions such as mandatory minimums and sentencing guidelines diminish the discretionary authority of judges, thereby increasing the discretionary power of prosecutors. A defendant's sentence under federal sentencing guidelines depends not only on the crimes of which the defendant is convicted but also the factual circumstances of the crime. The guidelines list certain exacerbating factors (such as "supervisory role in the offense" or "use of a weapon") that result in a higher sentence, and a few mitigating factors (such as "minor role in the offense" or "acceptance of responsibility" for the crime) that result in a lower sentence. The guidelines also permit downward *departures* for specified grounds (including cooperation) and authorize upward departures, again on grounds set forth in the detailed guideline system.

Plea bargaining in federal court thus often involves negotiation not only over which charges will be brought or dropped, but also over which facts about the crime and the offender will be brought to the sentencing judge's attention, and hence which sentencing guidelines will be applied. Fed. R. Crim. P. 11(e)(1)(B). If the government and defense counsel have negotiated an agreement as to both the charges and the factual circumstances of the offenses, they have effectively determined what sentence the defendant will receive, leaving the judge with little sentencing discretion. And where the defendant and the prosecution have not agreed on the factual circumstances, the burden on the government to prove exacerbating factors is only a "preponderance of the evidence" rather than the "proof beyond a reasonable doubt" standard that applies to the proof of the elements of crimes.

Once a plea has been negotiated, a formal proceeding, the *guilty plea hearing*, is held. Fed. R. Crim. P. 11. At the hearing, a federal judge makes an effort to ensure that the defendant is entering the guilty plea voluntarily, knowingly, and without coercion. To do so, the judge informs a defendant of the nature of the charges that would have had to be proven, of the rights not to plead guilty and to have the case decided by a jury, and of the maximum sentence that might be imposed. The court typically requires some information from the prosecution, and sometimes from the defendant, so that a record can be made of the *factual basis* for the plea. (Note that the judge does not require proof beyond a reasonable doubt, as would be required at trial.) A guilty plea hearing occurs in open court, with all parties, counsel, and a court reporter present.

If plea negotiations are unsuccessful, or while they are taking place, prosecution and defense prepare for trial. As in civil actions, defendants may attack the initiating documents as defective; defendants may seek to have indictments dismissed (sometimes called motions to *quash* or *demurrers*) because of various defects including the failure to indict in the proper jurisdiction, prosecutorial misconduct, violations of grand jury secrecy, and the like. Fed. R. Crim. P. 12. Defendants may also request further specificity (a *bill of particulars*), severance of counts or co-defendants, suppression or exclusion of specific evidence, or discovery of grand jury materials. Certain objections, if not made at the appropriate pretrial stage, are waived. All of these motions may provide defendants with information about the prosecution's case.

Two important differences between criminal and civil pretrial practice are the statutory time limits on the criminal pretrial process and the much more limited scope of discovery in criminal cases. In terms of time limits, the Sixth Amendment guarantees criminal defendants the right to a speedy trial, and a federal statute (the Speedy Trial Act of

1974, 18 U.S.C. §§ 3161–3174) sets forth specific time constraints. Because of the Speedy Trial Act's requirements, criminal cases take priority over civil cases on federal court calendars. Some criminal defense attorneys argue that the relatively brief time from filing of indictment to trial works to the prosecution's advantage, since the prosecution has had all the pre-indictment time for investigation of the case whereas the defendant may only have learned of the case at the time of indictment. The prosecution/defense disparity is further exacerbated because, prior to the indictment, the prosecution has had the assistance of law enforcement officials and the grand jury.

As to the amount of information formally required to be exchanged before trial, criminal discovery is more restricted than the civil disclosure/civil discovery system. As noted, on the civil side, since the late 1930s, witness lists, experts' opinions, and underlying documents have generally been available to opponents. In contrast, on the criminal side, the rules do not mandate expansive disclosure; the exchange of witness lists, the taking of depositions, and the like are exceptional, rather than commonplace, events.

Two justifications are frequently offered. One is a fear that if defendants knew of information, they would either do harm to or attempt to tamper with witnesses or evidence. The other is that, given defendants' Fifth Amendment constitutional protections from self-incrimination, each side would not have the same obligations of disclosure. Some states do, within the confines of the Fifth Amendment, require forms of reciprocal discovery.

Further, both informal and formal discovery techniques do exist in criminal cases. Some prosecution offices maintain open files and give ready access to information. Under Supreme Court interpretations of the Due Process Clause, the prosecution is obliged to provide defendants with exculpatory information (*Brady materials,* named after the case which announced the rule). However, the prosecution (rather than the defendant or the court) determines what data fit that description, and disclosure failures may never come to light or, if discovered, may not be found to be sufficiently grave as to require reversal of convictions. In addition, a federal statute (the Jencks Act, 18 U.S.C. § 3500) requires that prosecutors provide the defense (upon its motion) with the prior statements of witnesses, but only if those witnesses testify at trial. Moreover, only statements that relate to the witness's testimony at trial must be produced. See also Fed. R. Crim. P. 26.2 (incorporating the Jencks Act's requirements into the Federal Rules and adding an obligation that the defense provide prior statements of its witnesses to the prosecution).

The Federal Rules of Criminal Procedure also provide that notices of alibis and of insanity defenses must be provided (Fed. R. Crim. P. 12.1 and 12.2). In exceptional cases, depositions may be taken (Fed. R. Crim. P. 15). Rule 16 requires that the government provide the defendant with her or his own prior statements, and with information about his or her prior record. In certain circumstances, the government must permit the defendant to inspect documents, including all documents that the government plans to introduce at trial. Once the defendant seeks certain kinds of discovery from the government, the defendant must respond in kind, subject to claims of privilege, the most obvious being the Fifth Amendment protection against self-incrimination. In some instances, because of the limited scope of discovery, defendants may try to use the pretrial motion process and preliminary hearings as a means of obtaining information about the government's case. Either party can request a pretrial conference, or the court may *sua sponte* (on its own) order a pretrial conference.

Turning to criminal trials, of the some 6,700 that occurred in federal court in the year 2000, juries and judges each decided about half. Under the Sixth Amendment, criminal defendants have a right to trial by jury within the locality (or vicinage) where the crime occurred. See also Fed. R. Crim. P. 18, 21, and 23. The jury and vicinage rights apply in state and federal court because the Supreme Court has interpreted the Fourteenth Amendment to incorporate these Sixth Amendment guarantees. (In contrast, the Court has held that neither the Seventh Amendment right to a jury in civil cases nor the Sixth Amendment grand jury provisions apply to the states.) When jury rights are exercised, presiding judges examine prospective jurors, and, as in civil cases, the parties may request that specific questions be asked. Currently, in the federal system judges ask questions for the voir dire, but in many states, attorneys directly question prospective jurors. As in the civil system, parties can challenge prospective jurors for cause or peremptorily. Fed. R. Crim. P. 24. In federal criminal cases, the jury is composed of twelve people; state juries range from six to twelve. In exceptional cases, juries are "sequestered," that is, kept apart from family and community during the case to prevent them from learning prejudicial information. The government must establish its case beyond a reasonable doubt, and the verdict in federal cases (and in all but two states) must be unanimous. Fed. R. Crim. P. 31. More on juries can be found in Chapter VI.

During criminal trials, motions to dismiss (called motions for *judgment of acquittal*) can be made. Fed. R. Crim. P. 29. Defendants may seek dismissal of the case after the prosecution has presented its evidence, again after the defense has presented its case, and again after the jury or judge has returned its verdict. In order to prevail, the defendant must show that the "evidence is insufficient to sustain a verdict." Prosecutors cannot, in contrast, make a parallel motion; no directed verdict can be obtained by the government. If the defendant's motions are denied, closing arguments are held, juries instructed by judges, and verdicts rendered. If a jury has questions, it may send notes to the judge, who must inform the parties of the jury's questions and the court's responses. If the jury has difficulty reaching a verdict and so informs the court, a judge may call the jury back into court and recharge them, urging them to work out a verdict. This charge is sometimes referred to as an *Allen* or *dynamite* charge and in some jurisdictions, it is not permitted. If the jury can still not agree (a *hung jury*), then a mistrial is declared, and retrial may occur at the prosecution's discretion. If a jury finds a defendant not guilty, the government may not, under current readings of the Double Jeopardy Clause, appeal. Defendants can appeal verdicts of guilt. 28 U.S.C. § 1291.

C. After Conviction: Sentencing, Appeals, and Post-Conviction Relief

After a conviction is obtained either by guilty plea, nolo plea, or trial, the court sets a date to impose sentence.

During the 1980s, the federal sentencing system and that of many states shifted from one in which judges had a wide range of discretion to one in which judicial discretion is greatly reduced. Before that time, statutes often provided for a range of penalties (e.g., 1 to 10 years); judges were supposed to individualize a sanction in light of the particular characteristics of a defendant and the offense. Appeals of sentences were generally unavailable. Parole opportunities existed, permitting release if permitted by parole boards. Parole boards sometimes reviewed inmates' behavior during confinement but often served as a second institution to impose sentence, reassessing culpability. Statutory *good time* enabled inmates to reduce the amount of time they had to serve if they complied with prison rules.

Concerns about inequalities and "truth in sentencing" prompted many to seek reform. In 1984, Congress framed a different system, in which the United States Sentencing Commission (comprised of seven voting members, including three federal judges, and one nonvoting member) promulgated *guidelines* providing proposed ranges of months to be served depending on a defendant's offense level and criminal history. See 28 U.S.C. §§ 991–998. Sentencing decisions occur after an abbreviated factfinding process relying on a lower standard of proof than does a criminal trial. The court may consider evidence that is inadmissible at trial so long as it has "probable accuracy." See U.S. Sentencing Guidelines Manual § 6A1.3(a). As noted, judges may depart upward or downward from the guidelines on specified grounds. Sentencing decisions are now subject to appeal by either the prosecution or defense. 28 U.S.C. § 3742. Under the reforms, parole in the federal system was phased out.

Prior to the imposition of sentence, the United States Department of Probation (a part of the judicial branch) researches the circumstances of the crime and of the defendant and files a *presentence report* with the judge. Fed. R. Crim. P. 32. The sentencing court and the United States Bureau of Prisons rely upon information in that document when making decisions. Under Rule 32, the *presentence* report must be provided to the defendant or his or her attorney, who are promptly supposed to request corrections. Thereafter, relying on the presentence report and after a hearing to resolve factual conflicts between the versions of the case provided by the government and the defendant, the court imposes sentence pursuant to the federal sentencing guidelines.

At the time of sentencing, the defendant has the right to be present in court and to address the judge (referred to as the *right of allocution*). Fed. R. Crim. P. 32. In addition, under the Victim's Protection and Compensation Act of 1982, *victim impact statements* must be provided to the sentencing court, and judges are to consider restitution to the victim. 18 U.S.C. §§ 3556 et seq. Thus, although not technically a party to the criminal action, a victim may sometimes recover lost property or damages for physical injuries. In addition to restitution, sentences may range from probation and fines to incarceration for many years to life. Some states, and more recently the federal system, also authorize imposition of the death penalty. Capital punishment was once the province of either judge or jury, but under Supreme Court mandates, if predicated on facts that are elements of the underlying offence, is now the responsibility of the jury. See Ring v. Arizona, 536 U.S. 584 (2002). Separate sentencing proceedings are often held in capital cases, which, in many jurisdictions, also include a mandatory appeal.

Another possibility is the *suspended sentence*, under which a defendant is sentenced to a term of imprisonment but the sentence is suspended and the defendant placed on probation, under supervision by a probation officer. Upon certain kinds of misbehavior, the original sentence may be executed and the defendant incarcerated. The places of incarceration range from community treatment centers or halfway houses to maximum security institutions.

Some defendants are kept in custody from the moment of arrest through trial, while others are released on bail. 18 U.S.C. § 3141. After conviction, bail may be continued or revoked, pending sentencing or appeal. The 1984 bail reforms made post-conviction bail more difficult to obtain. Detention is required unless the court finds by "clear and convincing evidence that the person is not likely to flee or pose a danger" and that the appeal "is not filed for purpose of delay and raises a substantial question of law or fact likely to result in reversal or an order for a new trial." 18 U.S.C. § 3143. Bailed but convicted defendants, sentenced to incarceration, may be permitted to *self report* (i.e., surrender themselves) to prison or may have to surrender to federal authorities at the time of sentencing.

As in civil cases, criminal defendants may try to have judgments against them altered. Within seven days of a verdict, a defendant may request a new trial on various grounds. Requests based upon newly discovered evidence can be made until three years after judgment. Fed. R. Crim. P. 33. Defendants may also ask for "arrest" of judgment for errors (Fed. R. Crim. P. 35), for "correction or reduction of sentence" (Fed. R. Crim. P. 35), or for vacation of sentence. 28 U.S.C. § 2255 and the Rules Governing Section 2255 Proceedings in United States District Court. In addition, defendants—but not prosecutors—may appeal judgments of guilt. As noted, the constitutional prohibition on Double Jeopardy limits the prosecution's ability to appeal convictions as contrasted with sentences. The government cannot appeal an acquittal, but it can appeal judgments dismissing indictments and directing verdicts of acquittal.

The Federal Rules of Appellate Procedure govern the appellate process in both civil and criminal cases and provide that defendants must file a criminal appeal within ten days, while the prosecution has thirty days in which to file. Fed. R. App. P. 4. On appeal, certain issues not raised at trial will not be considered unless *plain error* (an extraordinary mistake affecting substantial rights) is found. Fed. R. Crim. P. 52. Defects not affecting *substantial rights* are deemed *harmless* and are insufficient bases for reversing convictions. The evidence is viewed in the light most favorable to the prosecution. In criminal cases as in civil cases, after appeal, review may also be sought in the United States Supreme Court by writ of certiorari.

After all appellate avenues are exhausted, prisoners may be able to request reconsideration of convictions by virtue of the constitutional right of *habeas corpus*, based upon the common law writ used to test the legality of a detention. Federal statutes implement the process, providing somewhat different routes for federal and state prisoners. For those convicted in federal court, "2255 motions," filed under 28

U.S.C. § 2255, bring defendants back to the judge who imposed sentence to ask that judge to set aside a conviction or a sentence on the grounds that it was obtained in violation of federal rights. State prisoners may also seek review in federal court of state court convictions on grounds that convictions or sentences violate federal constitutional law. Their applications, filed under 28 U.S.C. § 2254, can be considered only after state remedies have been exhausted. In addition, many other doctrines limiting federal court review have been codified and expanded by the Antiterrorism and Effective Death Penalty Act of 1996 (AEDPA). Judicial reconsideration is strictly limited, even when innocence is asserted as grounds or when the application of the death penalty is in issue.

Most prisoners present their applications for post-conviction review pro se. Counsel is not routinely provided because the Constitution has not been interpreted to require lawyers for post-conviction proceedings. Some statutes do provide for counsel in post-conviction hearings. An example is a provision for federally-funded assistance when certain challenges are made to the death penalty.

In 1977, specific rules came into effect to govern the procedure for state and federal post-conviction requests. See the Rules Governing Section 2254 and Section 2255 Proceedings in the United States District Courts. Under these rules, courts review filings prior to the service on the government. Further, special rules for waiving filing fees exist; in general, prisoners have to pay nominal amounts. See 28 U.S.C. § 1915(a). The rules governing Section 2254 applications and Section 2255 motions permit limited discovery, only upon court order. The rules also authorize courts to hold evidentiary hearings in appropriate cases. Most of the cases, however, are disposed of on the papers. Relatively few prisoners request such relief, and far fewer succeed in convincing courts to reconsider and void convictions. Unsuccessful litigants at the trial court may seek review in higher courts and in the United States Supreme Court.

III. Choosing the Law to Apply and Exercising Power over People

Whether proceeding as an individual or as an aggregate action, and whether parties come from the same or more than one jurisdiction, courts have to decide what law to apply and to which persons their authority extends. Proceduralists thus have to understand the structure of arguments about choosing legal regimes and about courts' territorial reach.

Questions of application of law arise for both substantive rules of conduct and the procedural rules that govern the interactions among disputants, witnesses, and judges. Given those many layers and the overlap between procedure and substance, readers will not be surprised to learn that problems of *choice of law*, sometimes assumed to be *conflicts of law*, have engaged jurists for centuries.

A central proposition is that no matter what the forum (public courts or private decisionmaking tribunals, domestic or international), a question exists about what law to apply. Further, courts and dispute resolution processes may draw upon more than one source of law within a given dispute to resolve different questions—from process and evidentiary rules to liability and damage measures.

For example, both state and federal systems routinely look to their counterparts to decide what law applies but the statutes and doctrines guiding the application of law have not always required the same results. Specifically, before 1938, federal courts generally used the procedural rules of the state in which they sat. After 1938, federal courts used a national set of rules—the Federal Rules of Civil Procedure, which displaced most (but not all) state procedural rules. In contrast, until 1938, in cases within federal court authority through diversity jurisdiction (involving citizens from different states with an amount in controversy sufficient for statutory requirements), federal courts understood themselves to have the power to determine the substantive liability rules by developing common law when necessary.

But, in 1938, the Supreme Court decided Erie Railroad Co. v. Tompkins, 304 U.S. 64 (1938), and concluded that federal courts had, when the cause of action arose under state law, to apply state law. The *Erie* rule, announced just as a national federal procedural system came into being, prompted many questions about whether a particular federal rule ought not to be used in a diversity action because it had such an effect on the outcome that it undermined the requirement of using state "substantive" law. That formulation resembled the congressional charter for federal courts to make procedural rules—requiring such rules not to "abridge, enlarge or modify any substantive right." 28 U.S.C. § 2072(b).

Over subsequent decades, many challenges to the application of federal rules followed. Justices have offered various formulations (such as whether a rule was "outcome determinative" or "outcome affective," whether a rule was properly categorized as "procedural" or "substantive," or whether application of a particular rule would "substantially affect primary decisions respecting human conduct") to attempt to delineate the scope of federal procedural rulemaking from state-power over liability standards. In general, the Court has confirmed the capacity for national procedural rules to embrace claims arising under either state or federal law, but litigants need to attend to the possibility that a state rule could be characterized as both procedural and substantive (such as appellate standards to limit damages awarded by jurors or the method for calculating when a statute of limitations has been tolled) and that it may be applied in federal court.

Assume for the moment that a legal question—such as whether a property owner ought to be liable to trespassers for injuries caused by negligence or only for those injuries caused willfully—is readily understood as substantive and hence that federal courts must, under *Erie*, use state law. Another question exists: which state law is to be applied?

That same question arises any time two litigants in dispute come from different jurisdictions. When people in dispute come with political or physical affiliations with more than one polity, what law ought to govern a dispute? The general justifications for applying a forum's law to a person is that the person has so agreed—sometimes implicitly through physical presence in a jurisdiction, sometimes constructively through benefitting from the laws of a jurisdiction, and sometimes expressly or implicitly by being a member of a polity and theoretically giving political consent to its law. But when people make such implicit or explicit agreements with different jurisdictions that in turn have different liability rules, what ought decisionmakers ruling on a dispute to do?

Again, the answers have not been constant. One possibility is that disputants agree, ex ante, to the regime of law to govern disputes. Contracts often specify what law applies to conflicts that emerge. Absent such agreements, courts have devised a range of approaches. For some, the place in which the dispute arose becomes a touchstone. As is obvious, in a world in which many transactions span a wide geographic expanse, litigants can disagree about which place is the relevant one.

Moreover, even when an event occurred in a specific locale, that place may otherwise have very little to do with the disputants. For example, assume parties to a contract meet in an airport in Chicago to sign an agreement, but the underlying activities take place in California and New York. Or that an accident occurs in Canada, but passengers and drivers from both cars come from New York and return to New York for care and treatment. Or that a car, driven by people en route to Arizona, catches fire in Oklahoma, but the claim is that the manufacturer in Germany or the importer and seller in New York caused the defect that resulted in the fire. Such cases prompted courts to consider the "center of gravity" or the place that had "significant contacts" with a conflict as more appropriate sources of law.

Within the United States, constitutional provisions inform the discussion. The Supreme Court has concluded that, as a matter of due process, courts may not use law from a jurisdiction that has no relationship with the underlying conflict or the disputants. Currently, the formulation is that a jurisdiction's law can only be applied if that jurisdiction has either a significant contact or a sufficient aggregation of contacts as to make the application of its law neither "arbitrary nor fundamentally unfair." Allstate Insurance Co.

v. Hague, 449 U.S. 302 (1981). Moreover, when aggregate litigation is ongoing, courts may be required to disaggregate the conflict, applying different states' liability rules to subsets of litigants. See Phillips Petroleum Co. v. Shutts, 472 U.S. 797 (1985).

A second relevant constitutional provision is the Full Faith and Credit clause of Article IV, requiring that each state give full faith and credit to the "public Acts, Records, and judicial Proceedings of every other state" and that Congress prescribe implementing laws. Congress has done so, as well as requiring that federal courts give full faith and credit to state and territorial court proceedings. See 28 U.S.C. § 1738. That provision has been read to require that a court has to accord the same weight and finality to a judgment as would the issuing jurisdiction, but only when a judgment is final. As a consequence, Congress has made different rules for inter-state coordination of orders such as child custody and support that are typically modifiable because of changing circumstances. See, e.g., 28 U.S.C. §§ 1738A, 1738B. Congress has also made specific rules exempting certain state acts from having preclusive effect in other jurisdictions. An example is the Defense of Marriage Act (DOMA), 28 U.S.C. § 1738C.

The effect of the Full Faith and Credit statutes and constitutional premise is not always clear or easy and, as DOMA illustrates, the issue is how substantial policy decisions made in one jurisdiction affect others. The increasing mobility of persons and goods, coupled with the ability to litigate issues repeatedly in different jurisdictions, make for yet additional complexity. For example, if a court approves a settlement in one jurisdiction that includes an agreement by a disputant not to testify against the other, can another state have the power, at the behest of new litigants, to issue a subpoena to one of the original disputants as a witness? Baker v. General Motors, 522 U.S. 222 (1998), with facts akin to that example, produced several opinions struggling to delineate permissible and impermissible enforcement of the first jurisdiction's order.

This example also suggests the larger problem: How broad a reach ought legal rules have? The term universal jurisdiction is used to denote that certain violations of norms transcend the boundaries of a given jurisdiction. A commitment to shared norms of behavior—supra positive norms—has been used to permit a country that lacks any physical ties to a conflict to exercise jurisdiction in the hopes of providing a measure of justice that would otherwise be unavailable. Offenses such as slave trade, genocide, and war crimes are examples of those recognized as providing a basis for universal jurisdiction. Domestic courts sometimes exercise civil or criminal jurisdiction on that basis. Alternatively, international tribunals (discussed in Chapter V) can be created to provide an infrastructure outside the nation-state to respond.

Another point bears noting: jurisdiction here means the power to impose law but it may also refer to the power to require the attendance of defendants. Given the size of the United States, the increasingly national and international network of communications and industry, and the existence of quasi-sovereign states, the problem of where to try a given case arises with some frequency both locally and globally. Jurisdiction over the person of the plaintiff is not often an issue because the plaintiff volunteers to appear in a particular court by filing the complaint. Aggregate litigation provides an exception. For example, in class actions, issues also exist about jurisdiction over absent class members who have not themselves volunteered to enter a particular court system. In general, however, the focus is on reaching defendants.

Both subject matter and personal jurisdiction are needed for a court to proceed. In the United States, while some had argued that issues of subject matter jurisdiction had to be resolved first, a unanimous Supreme Court concluded in Ruhrgas AG v. Marathon Oil Co., 526 U.S. 574 (1999), that federal courts have discretion to address the questions in either order, as both are requisite to proceeding. Remember that as a general matter, federal courts do not exercise nation-wide jurisdiction over defendants, but are limited by the state boundaries in which the federal courts sit.

Sometimes the two forms of jurisdiction are closely related. For example, federal criminal subject matter jurisdiction extends to crimes committed in or affecting the United States, and jurisdiction over defendants comes from having physical authority over the defendant. Unlike civil actions in which civil defendants can be served outside the jurisdiction in which the case is filed, in criminal cases in federal courts (unlike the practice in some foreign countries and some states), the physical presence of a defendant is generally required at most phases of the criminal felony process, from arraignment through sentencing. However, a federal prosecution is not totally dependent on the physical presence of a defendant. Indictments can be filed no matter where a defendant is, and once a trial is commenced, a defendant who voluntarily leaves or is disruptive may be tried in her or his absence. Nevertheless, on the criminal side, as on the civil side, personal and subject matter jurisdiction can be distinguished. The federal government could have physical custody of a defendant but not be able to charge her or him because a crime falls outside federal criminal subject matter jurisdiction. For example, a theft that does not involve interstate commerce is typically not a federal crime. Alternatively, the federal government could have subject matter jurisdiction over a crime but, because a defendant has left the jurisdiction, the government may not be able to prosecute—absent extradition (or kidnapping).

A body of Supreme Court decisions deals with the problem of state or federal courts exercising jurisdiction over parties who are neither residents nor citizens of the place where they are sued and who sometimes are physically absent from a jurisdiction when a proceeding is commenced. All these cases face the question of the relationship between territorial boundaries and the legitimacy of the exercise of jurisdiction.

Pennoyer v. Neff, 95 U.S. 714 (1877), decided soon after the Civil War, provides insight into the history and the effects of politics and of technology on legal rules. The case involved two interrelated lawsuits. In the first, filed in 1865, J. H. Mitchell, a lawyer and an Oregon resident, sued Marcus Neff, who was not in Oregon but who owned land in Oregon. The dispute was over attorney's fees; Mitchell claimed Neff owed him approximately $300.

At the time, Oregon law permitted plaintiffs to notify defendants of suits by mail (if addresses were known or could be found with reasonable diligence) or, if defendants owned property in Oregon, to provide notice by publication. In this case, because Mitchell did not know Neff's address, Mitchell "notified" Neff of the pending lawsuit by publishing a notice for six successive weeks in the county's weekly newspaper, the Pacific Christian Advocate. Neff did not appear, a default judgment was entered against him, and the property was sold at a sheriff's sale to Mitchell, who thereafter assigned it to Sylvester Pennoyer.

The second case, commenced in 1874 between Pennoyer and Neff, was a dispute over who owned the property. If, in the first action, the judgment against Neff were valid, then, in the second action, Pennoyer would hold title. But, if the Mitchell v. Neff default judgment was invalid, then Pennoyer's claim of ownership would fail.

The United States Supreme Court held that the default judgment was unconstitutional because the lawsuit, involving personal obligations between the parties, had commenced without personally serving a defendant within the state's borders. Justice Field explained:

> The authority of every tribunal is necessarily restricted by the territorial limits of the State in which it is established. Any attempt to exercise authority beyond those limits would be deemed in every other forum . . . an illegitimate assumption of power, and be resisted as mere abuse.

95 U.S. at 720. Given this premise, the Court concluded that Oregon courts had the power to regulate the conduct of the state's own citizens, to decide questions of civil status, to adjudicate the validity of contracts and the acquisition and disposition of property, both personal and real. But Oregon could not, without the consent of a non-resident, make those determinations about persons and property outside its borders.

In the case of Mitchell against Neff, Oregon did not have what the Court termed *in personam* jurisdiction over Neff because he did not reside within the State. While Oregon did have *in rem* jurisdiction over the issue of who owned land in Oregon, that question was not the basis of the Mitchell dispute. As the Court explained:

> Substituted service by publication ... may be suffi-
> cient to inform parties of the object of proceedings
> taken where property is once brought under the
> control of the court by seizure or some equivalent
> act. The law assumes that property is always in the
> possession of its owner, in person or by agent; and
> it proceeds upon the theory that its seizure will
> inform him, not only that it is taken into the
> custody of the court, but that he must look to any
> proceedings authorized by law upon such seizure
> for its condemnation and sale.

95 U.S. at 727. The failure in *Pennoyer* occurred, according
to the Court, because Mitchell had failed to "seize" Neff's
property at the commencement of the lawsuit; instead, the
seizure had occurred only *after* judgment had been entered
for Mitchell. Since judgments without jurisdiction are void,
and since, in Justice Field's view, jurisdiction over the person was wrapped up with adequate notice, Mitchell's suit
failed. In short, one could not obtain personal jurisdiction
over a nonresident defendant unless one served her or him
within the state.

The Court explained that its views were based upon a
theory of state sovereignty, in turn linked to territoriality.
Although states were not "in every respect independent," 95
U.S. at 722, the principles of "public law" applied to them.
Specifically, it was the "law" that

> every State possesses exclusive jurisdiction and sov-
> ereignty over person and property within its territo-
> ry. As a consequence, every State has the power to
> determine for itself the civil *status* and capacities of
> its inhabitants.... The several States are of equal
> dignity and authority, and the independence of one
> implies the exclusion of power from all others.

95 U.S. at 722–723. As a consequence, "[p]rocess from the
tribunals of one State cannot run into another State, and
summon parties there domiciled to leave its territory and
respond to proceedings against them." 95 U.S. at 727.

The Court also explained the relationship between its
opinion and the Due Process Clause of the Fourteenth
Amendment.

Since the adoption of the 14th Amendment to the Federal Constitution, the validity of such judgments may be directly questioned, and their enforcement in the State resisted, on the ground that proceedings in a court of justice to determine the personal right and obligations of parties over whom the court has no jurisdiction, do not constitute due process of law. . . .

95 U.S. at 733. Note that the decision is an early interpretation of the then-new Fourteenth Amendment.

The *Pennoyer* structure, with its due process analysis for determining whether a court may exercise jurisdiction over a defendant, endures in some respects—despite many transformations. In the United States, a court's authority is somehow tied to the boundaries of the state in which it sits. However, while notions of giving fair warning to the defendant of the pending lawsuit also enter into the consideration of the validity of judgments, the courts have come to understand notice and jurisdictional issues as two independent inquiries.

The logic of the *Pennoyer* structure was tested and strained in Harris v. Balk, 198 U.S. 215 (1905). Under *Pennoyer*, residents of one state could commence actions against non-residents by seizing property within the state and owned by the defendant. Thus, when a dispute arose between Epstein, a citizen of Maryland, and Balk, a North Carolinian, about the payment of $300 allegedly owed by Balk to Epstein, Epstein had a technique available to sue Balk in Maryland. Harris, also from North Carolina but temporarily in Maryland, owed Balk $180. Conceptualizing the $180 owed to Balk as Balk's "property" within Maryland, Epstein invoked the *Pennoyer* rule and attached that money by serving Harris. Thereafter, Balk sued Harris in North Carolina courts for the $180. Balk claimed that a debt did not "travel" with the debtor but remained with the creditor; under this view, the $180 owed to Balk remained "in" North Carolina. Thus, Balk had no property "in" Maryland, and therefore Harris' payment to Epstein did not discharge the debt owed Balk. Balk won in the North Carolina courts but lost in the United States Supreme Court.

The Court concluded that the question of jurisdiction could not be made to "depend on the so-called original situs of the debt.... Power over the person of the garnishee confers jurisdiction on the courts of the State where the writ issues...." 198 U.S. at 222–223. The Court further held that, in general, once a debt was attached, the debtor had the obligation to provide notice of the pendency of the action to the creditor, who would thus be afforded an opportunity to protest.

Consider the implications of the *Pennoyer* and *Balk* holdings. If such a defendant entered the state, then she or he would be personally liable for the full amount sought, since, under *Pennoyer,* power to adjudicate flowed from a defendant's physical presence within a state's borders. Alternatively, if a defendant did not enter the state, she or he risked default in the amount of the property attached.

To respond to these problems, the courts created a device described as a *special* or *limited appearance* which permitted a defendant to enter a state for the sole purpose of contesting the validity of the jurisdiction. If successful, the suit was dismissed. If unsuccessful, the defendant retained the option to leave the state, to default up to the limits of the property attached, but to risk no more than that amount. All that was adjudicated in such a case was the defendant's liability up to the limits of the property. As a consequence, if a plaintiff sought to obtain more than that amount, the plaintiff would have to go to the defendant's state, commence a new suit, and litigate the merits of the claim.

Think about the case of a farmer in Lancaster, Pennsylvania, who drove a horse-drawn buggy and who had never traveled further than 20 miles from his home. What happened when he was hit by a car, driven by a citizen of Massachusetts? Under the *Pennoyer* rules, would the farmer have to travel to Massachusetts to file suit? The courts kept physical presence as the touchstone but responded with the fiction that a proposed defendant had appointed the Secretary of State as an agent to accept service of process within the state seeking to exercise jurisdiction.

With such modifications, the *Pennoyer–Balk* rules endured for almost seventy years. In 1945, however, the Supreme Court announced a major inroad into the *Pennoyer* presence-equals-power-rule. That case was International Shoe Co. v. State of Washington, 326 U.S. 310 (1945), in which Washington sought to compel contributions from International Shoe to the state's unemployment compensation program. Employers were supposed to make contributions to the state unemployment compensation fund. Washington provided notice of the delinquency proceeding by having papers served personally upon a sales solicitor employed by International Shoe in Washington and by sending a copy of the papers to the corporate headquarters in St. Louis via registered mail. The dispute was over (1) whether International Shoe had to defend in Washington and (2) whether International Shoe was an "employer" who had to contribute to the fund.

International Shoe was a Delaware corporation, its principal place of business was in St. Louis, and its merchandise was distributed through sales units located outside Washington. In Washington, the company at no time employed more than 13 salespersons, who were directly supervised by the St. Louis office. The salespersons' authority was limited to showing samples (of single shoes) and soliciting orders which they then transmitted to St. Louis for acceptance or rejection. No salesperson had the authority to enter into contracts or to make collections. The state court in Washington upheld the state's jurisdiction and assessed the back taxes. The defendant obtained United States Supreme Court review. The question in *International Shoe* was whether the State of Washington could, consistent with the Fourteenth Amendment, subject the company to its jurisdiction.

In *International Shoe,* the Supreme Court held that the "presence" test of *Pennoyer* no longer governed all of the rules of personal jurisdiction:

> Whether due process is satisfied must depend rather upon the quality and nature of the activity in relation to the fair and orderly administration of the laws which it was the purpose of the due process clause to insure. That clause does not contemplate that a State may make binding a judg-

ment in personam against an individual or corporate defendant with which the State has no contacts, ties, or relations.

326 U.S. at 319–320. The Court also upheld service of process on an agent for the corporation and stated further: "[n]or can we say that the mailing of the notice of suit to appellant by registered mail at its home office was not reasonably calculated to apprise appellant of the suit." 326 U.S. at 320.

As discussed by the Court in more recent opinions, *International Shoe* marked the beginnings of the "reasonableness test." Chief Justice Stone's opinion for the Court stated that the inquiry was to focus upon whether there have been

> such contacts of the corporation with the state of the forum as make it reasonable, in the context of our federal system of government, to require the corporation to defend the particular suit which is brought there.

326 U.S. at 317. As Justice Marshall, in Shaffer v. Heitner, 433 U.S. 186, 204 (1977) later explained, under the rules provided by *International Shoe*: "The relationship among the defendant, the forum, and the litigation, rather than the mutually exclusive sovereignty of the States on which the rules of *Pennoyer* rest, became the central concern of the inquiry into personal jurisdiction."

The next landmark in the jurisprudence of jurisdiction occurred in 1950, with the Supreme Court's decision in Mullane v. Central Hanover Bank & Trust, 339 U.S. 306 (1950). *Mullane* established that the question of whether notice was constitutionally sufficient was distinct from the question of whether a court had jurisdiction over the person of a defendant. As a consequence, two independent due process inquiries were necessary when a challenge was made to a court's jurisdiction. First, a judge had to determine whether the notice provided a defendant was "reasonably calculated, under all the circumstances, to apprise interested parties of the pendency of the action and afford them an opportunity to present their objections." 339 U.S. at 314. Second, a judge had to determine whether it was fair and just to exercise jurisdiction over the defendant and that, in turn, depended upon the strength of the state's interests and its customary character.

These new rules applied to "in personam" civil jurisdiction cases but the question of what rules applied to so-called "in rem" cases persisted. In 1977, in Shaffer v. Heitner, 433 U.S. 186 (1977), the Court addressed that issue. Delaware had a statute that permitted the seizure of stock of Delaware corporations as the basis for asserting jurisdiction over defendant stockholders in the Delaware courts. Justice Marshall, writing for the Court, first noted that the in rem/in personam dichotomy was misleading; jurisdiction over "things" was really adjudication over individuals' interests in "things." Thereafter, he concluded that the same test applied to all forms of jurisdiction: "all assertions of State court jurisdiction must be evaluated according to the standards set forth in *International Shoe* and its progeny." 433 U.S. at 212.

International Shoe, Mullane, and *Shaffer* marked the transition from the *Pennoyer* territorial basis for jurisdictional rules to rules premised upon notions of fairness. However, while territorial sovereignty notions have been eclipsed, they have not been obliterated. When defendants are physically present in states, the Court has concluded that service on them suffices to establish jurisdiction over them. See Burnham v. Superior Courts, 495 U.S. 604 (1990). Moreover, state boundaries still provide the basis for arguments over jurisdiction in civil cases, and a "physical presence test" has some vitality in criminal cases. And, moving to a test that invokes fairness—which in turn may be connected to or partially dependent upon state borders—does not decide the questions of whether, in this vast country, plaintiff or defendant must travel and why. As a consequence, the Supreme Court and lower courts have had numerous occasions to decide challenges to courts' jurisdictions. See World–Wide Volkswagen Corp. v. Woodson, 444 U.S. 286 (1980).

How do increasingly international interactions affect an understanding of what constitute affiliations that count for purposes of jurisdiction? What role ought the internet play? Is the web a new mechanism by which to affiliate with a particular jurisdiction? Does it alter what it means to be "in" a jurisdiction? Or is use of the web akin to the mailing of a letter, and as such, just another factor to be added to the analyses developed in the case law sketched above? Not surprisingly, commentators and courts have begun to address these issues, sometimes focused on how to deal with potential defendants outside of the United States and other times on new technologies of communication and transaction.

Illustrative is a draft of the Hague Convention on Jurisdiction and Foreign Judgments in Civil and Commercial Matters, modeled after the Brussels Convention on Jurisdiction and the Enforcement of Judgments in Civil and Commercial Matters, which applies among members of the European Union (EU). Some cases are seen to be easy. The infliction of tortious injury or the provision of goods and services are generally seen as proper bases for jurisdiction. More controversial are whether a defendant doing business in one jurisdiction can be subject to suit for activities unrelated to that business and whether physical presence alone can suffice.

Yet more controversial is the concept of "tag" jurisdiction, which while not novel to the United States and a part of English civil procedure, is a form of jurisdiction not readily embraced by the European Union. For example, in the Brussels Convention on the recognition and enforcement of foreign judgments, Article 3 requires that persons domiciled in a contracting state may only be sued in another state upon specific bases of personal jurisdiction affirmatively approved in the Convention. Examples include: a) domicile ("persons domiciled in a Contracting State shall, whatever their nationality, be sued in the courts of that State"); b) in contract cases, jurisdiction can arise "in the courts for the place of performance . . .;" c) "in matters relating to tort . . . in the courts for the place where the harmful event occurred." In contrast, Article 3 states that judgments founded on "temporary presence" of an individual are excluded from enforcement under the treaty.

Return once again to the notions of sovereignty and fairness to see how the two issues interrelate. Litigants' actions vis-a-vis a forum are used to justify a sovereign's exercise of jurisdiction? But what is the theory? One of implied contract? Consent? Benefits and burdens? Political power? Physical power? Moral force?

IV. REMEDIAL POWERS

Litigants turn to courts because they hope to achieve a particular outcome. People file cases not to have lawsuits but to bring about change outside the courthouse. And, courts have coercive power, or, as Robert Cover put it, the power to order violence in the name of the state. What then do courts have to offer as remedies?

I begin on the civil side, which has been dominated by two traditions: "legal" remedies and "equitable" remedies. The distinction between "law" and "equity" is a historical one that can be traced to the complex system of multiple jurisdictions that existed in England throughout the Middle Ages, the Renaissance, and beyond. Medieval England had many court systems, including admiralty, exchequer, baronial, and ecclesiastical courts.

Two English court systems came to assume special significance for the legal history of the United States: the common law courts, headed by Common Pleas and King's Bench and administering the common law of England, and the chancery courts, run by the Chancellor of England, the secretary of the King's cabinet who gradually assumed the authority to provide relief when the remedy "at law" was inadequate. At its inception, the Chancellor's exercise of remedial authority might have been truly extraordinary, but, over time, the Chancellor's work became routine as he administered a body of legal principles and rules that came to be known as *equity* and was distinguished from the rules and principles known as law (e.g., those applied by the courts of common law). Whole areas of law—such as the law of trusts—came to be the special creation and purview of the Chancellor.

In the United States, the distinction between law and equity can be found in the Constitution. The Seventh Amendment preserves the right of trial by jury in suits "at common law" when the amount in controversy exceeds $20. Many state constitutions provide similar or broader protection for jury decisionmaking. Further, some states developed separate courts for law and equity. In the federal system, until the 1930s, the courts used different systems of pleading and procedure for law and equity, although the same courts heard both sets of cases, sitting either as a court in law or equity.

During the twentieth century, however, the division between law and equity was, to some extent, bridged. As noted, in 1938, the federal courts moved to a uniform system of procedural rules for both kinds of cases: Rule 1 of the Federal Rules of Civil Procedure provides that those rules shall "govern the procedure . . . in all suits of a civil nature, whether cognizable as cases at law or in equity or in admiralty;" and Rule 2 announces a "single form" of civil action, abandoning both the distinction between legal and equitable actions and the common law variation, based on subject matter, among forms of action. For example, while equitable actions ended with a "decree" and legal actions with a "judgment" and appellate courts had different standards of review for each, the federal rules tried to meld the two systems into one. Some scholars argue that in the resultant mix, "equity" triumphed over "law" in that the rules provide judges with more discretion than judges had under the common law.

But given the constitutional protections of jury decisionmaking, founded on the intelligibility of certain cases being "suits at common law," and given sub-constitutional traditions of preferences for legal as contrasted with equitable remedies, the historical division between law and equity remains relevant to procedure, especially in discussions of courts' remedial authority. For example, when seeking the equitable remedy of an injunction, a showing is required that providing monetary damages (the common remedy at law) is inadequate. Moreover, recent Supreme Court decisions have, by narrow majorities, insisted on the limited equitable powers of federal judges.

Hence, consider first the role of damages in remedying injuries established through courts. Measuring the dollar value of an injury can on occasion be straightforward, as creditors seek repayments of specific debts. But frequently, assessing damages is more difficult, as questions need to be answered about how to decide what to count and then how to measure it. What kinds of losses should be included? Out-of-pocket expenses? Lost goodwill? The consequential losses resulting from the absence of an operating business? Should a plaintiff be restored to the position he or she would have occupied had the breach not occurred? Should emotional distress over the breach of contract be included in the damage calculation? Are only compensatory damages to be paid or may punitive damages, designed as a fine to punish the wrongdoer, also be awarded?

The problem of determining monetary damages in personal injury cases is especially difficult. How much is the loss of a leg worth? Ought the value be based on the loss as experienced by a specific person, his or her specific age, with his or her specific talents and interests and life expectations, or ought some less individualized metric be used? Should individuals be compensated for out-of-pocket expenses, such as medical care and lost wages, as well as for the pain and dislocation involved?

These questions have generated sustained controversies. For example, since the 1980s, with the growth of products liability, mass accidents, toxic torts, and consumer fraud litigation, large numbers of injured, similarly-situated victims have presented themselves to courts, often through aggregate proceedings such as class actions. The absolute dollar value of a relatively few judgments and many more settlements, and the attorneys' fees recovered, have been a focal point, prompting proposals for regulation. Critics attack some awards as windfalls and identify jury decisionmaking as the source of erratic and overly-generous awards. Proponents argue the system serves an important public interest, protecting individuals when regulations are either non-existent or insufficient.

One element of damages, pain and suffering, has drawn particular criticism. During the 1980s, in both federal and state legislatures, critics proposed caps on what they termed non-economic or "soft" damages, distinguishing medical expenses and lost wages (to be compensated without restrictions) from pain and suffering, emotional distress, and punitive damages (to be compensated up to a set amount, with statutory limits). Like the current tort system, those proposals rely upon a market-value based system in which the value of injuries is keyed to what a plaintiff (given her or his age,

race, sex, education) can command in the job market and
what medical care costs. Some federal legislation now includes such limitations, and many state statutes include caps
on the amount of money juries can award in certain kinds of
cases, such as medical malpractice claims. Further, some
statutes require that disputants first submit claims to specialized panels before a judge or jury can be involved.

Criticism of the damage system comes from a variety of
sources. Some social scientists worry that the damage award
system imposes high costs, in terms of money spent on
proof of liability and attorneys' fees, as compared to the
amount of dollars delivered in direct compensation to a
person injured. Others support the role of litigation as a
form of regulation but argue about its efficiency. Some
believe that reliance on lawyers as gatekeepers creates economically efficient incentives, and others argue that it results
in both over- and under-claiming. Other commentators are
concerned about the translation of human values into dollar
terms—that the commodification of injuries promotes little
by way of healing or social change. Some propose "alternative sanctions" that rely on apology or restitution. For some,
remedial processes based in courts limit the options, both
because of their coercive nature and because of their historical reliance on damages. These critics call for "alternative
dispute resolution" mechanisms, discussed below.

Turn now to equitable remedies, the use of which is
widespread. As noted, the issuance of an injunction requires
that irreparable harm exist and that no adequate remedy at
law be available. *Preventive injunctions* prohibit some discrete act or series of acts from occurring in the future;
reparative injunctions compel defendants to engage in a
course of conduct to correct the effects of past wrongs; and
structural injunctions attempt to reorganize ongoing social
institutions. Injunctions can be permanent but litigants may
also seek temporary, provisional remedies during a lawsuit,
such as a temporary restraining order, a preliminary injunction, or an order to freeze assets, all designed to maintain
the status quo pending the final outcome of a lawsuit.

From the 1960s through the end of the twentieth
century, courts have relied on structural injunctions to
respond to unconstitutional conditions in prisons, hospitals,

and schools. Beginning in the 1980s, judges developed other forms of structural relief in large scale tort cases, such as providing for "claims facilities" to decide the degree of injury and allocate funds to individuals injured by asbestos or other products.

Declaratory relief is somewhat akin to equitable relief. A declaratory judgment declares (rather than orders) the relationships of the parties or their respective rights. See 28 U.S.C. §§ 2201, 2202, and Fed. R. Civ. P. 57. Declaratory judgments may be sought when rights are unclear. An individual may be willing to abide by his or her legal obligation but may need a declaration to know what the obligation is. Because they rely on voluntary compliance, declaratory judgments are seen as less intrusive than injunctions. Rather than instruct a party to behave in a specific fashion, a court announces rights. However, if parties disobey, an opponent may return to court to obtain an injunction ordering the parties to abide by the declaratory judgment. In practice, litigants often ask for injunctive and declaratory relief at the same time. In some instances, they may ask for monetary damages as well.

A court's decision to require a given remedy may not conclude the lawsuit; parties do not always abide by court orders. In some circumstances, courts attempt to build enforcement or implementation mechanisms into their orders. For example, a monetary judgment may be accompanied by a schedule designed to enable a party to pay by staggering the times for payment. Some injunctions create auxiliary institutions, relying on committees, masters, or monitors to oversee implementation. Other orders appoint individuals to field complaints of non-enforcement or include provisions for arbitration or mediation of disputes arising under a decree.

Courts have several tools to enforce their judgments. When monetary damages are ordered but not paid, execution is available. A party's assets may be seized and sold or bank accounts or wages garnished to enforce the obligation to pay. If a party willfully disobeys an injunction, civil and criminal contempt are also available. Note that contempt is a sanction that can be imposed only for disobedience to a court order. Therefore, because declaratory judgments do not order defendants to follow a particular course of action, a litigant claiming a violation of a declaratory judgment must first request and obtain injunctive relief before being able to seek contempt.

Remedies in criminal cases include a comparable range of sanctions reflecting a variety of goals. The classic formulation of the principles justifying remedies in the criminal arena is that the sanctions imposed are to incapacitate, to deter (for the individual wrongdoer, specific deterrence, and for all others, general deterrence), to punish, and to rehabilitate. The relative significance of these goals varies over time, as one aspect is emphasized and another considered less salient. During the 1980s, another goal, victim compensation, gained prominence as the distinctions between criminal and civil processes diminished.

Legislatures have traditionally set the boundaries of criminal sanctions. They may stipulate that a particular crime is punishable by a fine not to exceed a certain amount as well as by a prison term of no more than a specified number of years. Legislatures may also decide whether a court can impose probation. Until recently, judges enjoyed substantial freedom to impose sentences within those statutory boundaries. However, as discussed in Chapter II, concern about crime control and disparate sanctions resulted in new laws of sentencing in both state and federal courts. Some laws provided mandatory minimum statutes, and others created guidelines that specified the time to be served. See, e.g., the Sentencing Reform Act of 1984, 18 U.S.C. §§ 3551 et seq. Those reforms have in turn resulted in new debates about over-incarceration of an aging and growing prison population.

Another area of controversy is the imposition of the death penalty. Some object to the imposition of capital punishment itself, arguing its unconstitutionality across a variety of dimensions. As with other kinds of sentences, concerns also include the problem of too much discretion for decisionmakers and too much variation in application. During the 1990s, "innocence projects" revisited the facts in some cases and identified defendants on death row who were factually innocent. Further, statistical studies continued to challenge the equality of the imposition of the death penalty. Many studies have shown that the race of both victims and assailants plays a significant role in death penalty decisionmaking. Thus far, the Supreme Court has refused to invalidate sentences based on such aggregate data and has limited challenges to proof of unconstitutional discrimination against a particular defendant.

Some remedies are used in both civil and criminal proceedings. One example is forfeiture, which derives from old English practices. A subject forfeited a "deodand" (the offending object) to the King as a penalty for violating the King's law. Forfeiture has evident utility as a penalty. If one deprives a wrongdoer of the instrument by which the harm occurred, the individual may lose the ability to repeat the bad act. In the United States, forfeiture statutes were enacted during Revolutionary and Civil War times and were used to prohibit enemies from retaining their assets.

In recent times, forfeiture proceedings have become increasingly popular as part of a strategy for combating organized crime, money laundering, and narcotics trafficking. Civil forfeiture proceedings are brought against the wrongdoing object, with cases having captions like United States v. 85 Reels of Film, United States v. $5800, or United States v. One 1998 Toyota Camry. These proceedings are civil lawsuits, but they often follow or are used in connection with criminal proceedings. Typically, the property that is the subject of the forfeiture is seized. Hearings are provided after seizure on the theory that prior notice gives a wrongdoer an opportunity to remove the property from a jurisdiction. When a person's home is at issue, however, the United States Supreme Court has concluded that only in urgent circumstances can the government proceed without notice and a hearing. In most federal forfeiture proceedings, the government establishes probable cause that the property is subject to forfeiture based on its use in committing or facilitating a crime. The burden then shifts to the person claiming the property, who must prove that he or she has legal title and that the property should not be forfeited. The grounds for avoiding forfeiture vary with the statutory basis for the forfeiture. For example, 19 U.S.C. § 1615 provides for forfeiture if customs laws are violated. Defenses include that the property owner exercised due care in entrusting an object to another.

Forfeiture law applies both to individuals who have been accused of violating laws and sometimes to third parties—those who own or possess property that others may have used for wrongdoing. Third parties have challenged forfeiture on due process grounds, but the Supreme Court has been reluctant to circumscribe substantially the use of forfeiture under the Fourteenth Amendment. For example, in 1996 a woman contested a state forfeiture statute on the ground that it did not permit a defense based on her being an innocent owner. The state had seized and sold the family car after her husband's conviction for engaging in sexual activity with a prostitute in the car, and his wife argued that she ought to have received money representing her economic interest in the vehicle. Relying on the deterrent purpose and the long history of forfeiture, the Court rejected her claim.

In 1970, pursuant to three statutes, Congress created a new form of forfeiture by authorizing government prosecutors to include forfeiture requests as part of criminal indictments. See The Controlled Substance Act, 21 U.S.C. § 801; The Bank Secrecy Act, 31 U.S.C. § 5317(c); and The Racketeering Influenced and Corrupt Organization Act (RICO), 18 U.S.C. § 1961. The government then pursued an active forfeiture policy. For example, in 1981, the Drug Enforcement Agency seized more than 1,300 cars, boats, and planes. In 1984, Congress passed the Comprehensive Crime Control Act of 1984, Pub. L. No. 98–473, 98 Stat. § 1837 (1984) (amending various sections of fifteen codes), and further expanded the availability of criminal forfeiture. The act also provided some procedural regularity for criminal forfeiture, such as bifurcating the forfeiture proceeding from the underlying criminal process. In practice, the inclusion of a forfeiture request in an indictment affects the incentives around plea bargaining. Controversy remained, and the Supreme Court has addressed questions of the effects of forfeiture proceedings on defendants' rights to counsel, to jury trials, and not to be subjected to double jeopardy. While often concluding that forfeiture proceedings were lawful, a specific forfeiture penalty was held in 1998 to violate the Excessive Fines Clause, for being "grossly dispro-portionate" to the gravity of the offense.

More recently, rulemakers addressed the criminal forfei-ture process, responding to some of the case law and criticisms by proposing an addition to the Criminal Rules—Rule 32.2, Criminal Forfeiture. The rule, effective in 2000, provides that: (1) an order of forfeiture will issue only if the defendant has been given notice of the forfeiture in the indictment or the information; (2) the court, and not the jury, is to determine whether or not the defendant's proper-ty is subject to forfeiture; (3) the government may seize the defendant's property prior to sentencing and after the court has entered a preliminary order of forfeiture; (4) civil mo-tions, such as motions to dismiss and motions for summary judgment, as well as discovery at the court's discretion, may be used in the ancillary hearing at which the interests of the defendant and any third-party claimants in the property are determined; (5) the court may stay the forfeiture of property pending appeal so that property may be returned to the defendant intact if the appeal is successful; and (6) the designation of property subject to forfeiture can be amend-ed upon motion.

The power of both civil and criminal sanctions stems in part from their finality, and thus a word is in order about how law provides for finality. Both courts and legislatures play a role, developing doctrines and practices that preclude repeated efforts to obtain relief based on the same underly-ing action. On the civil side, the terms *res judicata* and *collateral estoppel* mark that concept. On the criminal side, the Constitution ensures protection for criminal defendants by preventing repeated prosecution based on the same events; the shorthand is *double jeopardy*. But the interpreta-tion of what constitutes being "twice in jeopardy" has narrowed the constraint somewhat in practice. For example, in a case growing out of Prohibition, the Supreme Court concluded that a prosecution by one "sovereign" (i.e. a state) did not preclude a second prosecution based on the same events by another sovereign.

Interest in finality is cushioned by concern that, in some instances, reconsideration of orders is appropriate. One example is the existence of appellate structures, available in some but not all kinds of proceedings. For example, most small claims and arbitration proceedings are one-shot events, with no review permitted. In contrast, in some areas of law, reconsideration is directly built into a judgment. For example, child custody decisions are often structured to permit new arrangements due to changing circumstances. Further, injunctions can be modified based on changing circumstances. Sometimes statutes also specify limitations on the longevity of certain kinds of remedial orders. Moreover, when parole, "good time," habeas corpus, and pardon are available, criminal sanctions can also be reviewed in light of later developments.

For all the remedies described above, courts do not themselves have direct power to insist on compliance with their orders. Noncompliance is in fact a common problem, with examples including defendants failing to appear, parents failing to pay support orders, prison systems implementing mandated changes too slowly, and school systems refusing to obey desegregation orders. Implementation may be coerced through court orders such as contempt, but if force is required, courts must turn to the executive branch to provide law enforcement officials to carry out court orders. When judges craft remedial schemes, they are keenly aware of their dependence upon party cooperation to effectuate the results and upon the undesirability of seeking executive force to compel compliance. And litigants who seek remedies in court should also know the challenges of translating courts' orders into action.

V. INSTITUTIONAL FORMS

Legal proceedings take place within specific institutional structures. I now turn to those structures. Below, I describe some of the domestic tribunals (dominated by the federal and state courts, but including tribal courts, agency-based adjudication, and a variety of private or semi-private institutions) as well as international tribunals that are gaining in local influence as commercial and political transactions increasingly cross national borders.

A. Domestic Tribunals

Article III of the Constitution specifies the existence of the United States Supreme Court, leaves to Congress the creation of lower courts, and lists the subject matters over which federal courts have competence. Thus, the federal court structure is not fixed but changes over time with the addition of various tiers of decisionmakers. During much of the twentieth century, the federal system consisted of three tiers of courts: trial, intermediate appellate, and the Supreme Court. More recently, through creation of the positions of magistrate and of bankruptcy judges, the trial level has divided, such that a fourth tier has or is emerging.

Under Article III of the Constitution, the President, with the advice and consent of the Senate, appoints federal judges who have life tenure and guarantees of no diminution in salary. For clarity, I call these *constitutional judges*. As of 2000, about 650 federal district court judges, 170 appellate court judges, and the nine justices of the Supreme Court served in these positions. In addition, at the trial level, Congress has authorized two other sets of judges who sit inside Article III courts but who lack Article III attributes of life tenure. I call them *statutory judges*. As of 2000, about 315 bankruptcy judges and 450 magistrate judges served for renewable terms. Thus, the trial bench in the federal system has almost equal numbers of the two types of judges. All the federal courts are, as contrasted with the state courts, courts of *limited jurisdiction:* they may only hear cases over which

Congress or the Constitution has given the federal courts adjudicatory power.

Federal district courts are the trial courts, and are often described as courts of *original jurisdiction* because cases originate (come into the system) at that level and then proceed on to appellate courts. The geographic boundaries of the federal district courts' jurisdiction are coextensive with state court boundaries. Each state has at least one federal district court (e.g., the United States District Court for the District of Connecticut), and some of the larger states have four (e.g., the United States District Court for the Southern District of New York, the United States District Court for the Northern District of New York, the United States District Court for the Eastern District of New York, and the United States District Court for the Western District of New York). See 28 U.S.C. §§ 81 et seq. There are 94 federal district courts (including districts in the Virgin Islands, Puerto Rico, Guam, the Northern Mariana Islands, and the District of Columbia).

Each court, in turn, has at least one—and more commonly several—judges. See 28 U.S.C. §§ 132 et seq. As of 2000, the Southern District of New York was the largest court, with 28 authorized judgeships. In addition to the authorized judgeships, *senior judges* (who have served a certain minimum number of years and have reached a certain age, and who opt to free a place for a new Article III appointee) augment the working ranks. See 28 U.S.C. § 371. In most instances, trial judges preside singly, either with or without a jury; three-judge courts are now rare. See 28 U.S.C. § 2284. Given a caseload of about 260,000 civil and 60,000 criminal cases commenced yearly, district judges are assigned about 475 cases each.

Beginning in the late 1960s, federal courts have made increasing use of magistrate judges, who are appointed by federal district courts for eight year renewable terms and play many roles. Magistrate judges may rule on nondispositive motions, and in certain instances, may make dispositive rulings that are subject to review by a federal district judge. Further, with parties' consent, magistrate judges may preside at civil trials. In addition, in many jurisdictions, magistrate judges are assigned all habeas corpus cases and certain categories of civil cases, such as social security cases. The scope of their authority is set forth at 28 U.S.C. § 636. Magistrate judges have thus become a fourth tier of the judiciary, serving alongside a set of specialized judges who focus exclusively on bankruptcy. These bankruptcy judges are appointed by the appellate courts for 14 year renewable terms. With 1.3 million bankruptcies filed in 2000, the caseload per judge averaged about 4,000. See 28 U.S.C. §§ 151 et seq.

Yet other people work within the district courts, either as ad hoc participants or as full time staff. District judges have authority to appoint *special masters* in specific but unusual cases. Fed. R. Civ. P. 53. In addition, each judge has a staff that includes a secretary, a court clerk, and two or more law clerks (typically recent law school graduates who do legal research and drafting for judges). At the appellate level, additional personnel include a growing number of staff attorneys; in many circumstances, those staff attorneys screen cases. Note that magistrate judges, bankruptcy judges, special masters, staff attorneys, and law clerks are not appointed pursuant to Article III and do not enjoy the protections of life tenure and non-diminution of salary that are provided by the Constitution. Rather, they are regular employees of the courts, serve for renewable terms, and can be discharged for misconduct or neglect of duty. To discharge life tenured judges, in contrast, requires impeachment as provided by the Constitution.

The second-level court in the federal system is called a court of appeal and thirteen exist. Twelve federal appellate courts have jurisdiction over district courts within a specified territory, defined as including certain states. For example, the United States Court of Appeals for the Second Circuit hears cases from federal trial courts in New York, Connecticut, and Vermont; the Ninth Circuit hears cases from federal lower courts in Alaska, Arizona, California, Hawaii, Idaho, Montana, Nevada, Oregon, Washington, and Guam. See 28 U.S.C. §§ 41 et seq. The thirteenth, the Court of Appeals for the Federal Circuit, hears cases from all over the country relating to certain subject matters, predominantly patents and trademarks. See 28 U.S.C. § 1295.

Each appellate court consists of a varying number of active judges, ranging from about six to thirty. See 28 U.S.C. § 44. In 2000, 54,000 appeals were filed nationwide. About 10 to 20 percent of all appeals result in a published decision. Rates of publication vary by circuit and by judge. Three judges typically hear and rule on each appeal; fewer than three may decide motions filed with the court. In exceptional cases, an appellate court may sit *en banc,* in a group of all or of a majority of its active judges. See Fed. R. App. P. 35. Appellate courts may also authorize judges from outside the circuit or from district courts to sit on cases *by designation.* Thus, in practice, through the use of senior appellate judges (about 85 serving in 2000) and the designation of district judges (including some of the 270 senior district judges serving in 2000) who sit for a particular week or two, the appellate ranks are augmented significantly.

As in the trial courts, appellate courts are also aided by many non-Article III actors, including staff attorneys, law clerks, and lawyers who preside at conferences intended to induce settlement. The general right to appeal, a fixture for some 100 years, has been questioned of late because of the volume and expense of appeals. Some judges have proposed that appellate courts have certiorari-like power to choose what cases are reviewed. Some commentators argue that, with the growth of unwritten decisions and the decline in oral argument, appellate judges are in practice already picking which cases are reviewed fully.

In addition to the Court of Appeals for the Federal Circuit, the federal system has a few other specialized trial and appellate courts (such as the United States Court of International Trade and the United States Court of Federal Claims), some of which have been temporary and others of which are permanent. See, e.g., 28 U.S.C. §§ 251, 1491. Some of these specialized courts are staffed by constitutional judges, while others—such as the Tax Court—have judges appointed for fixed terms.

The highest court in the federal system is the United States Supreme Court, which sits in Washington, D.C. The Supreme Court is composed of nine justices, one Chief and eight associates, as fixed by 28 U.S.C. § 1. Except when a Justice recuses him or herself or is ill, all nine Justices participate in the decisionmaking in each case. In addition, each Justice is responsible for one or more of the circuits and sits to hear emergency motions from that circuit. The Supreme Court hears cases from both state and federal systems, but when it reviews cases from state courts it will only decide issues of federal law. As noted, most of the Court's docket is discretionary; four Justices are required to obtain a grant of certiorari. In addition to its appellate jurisdiction, the Supreme Court has a narrow *original jurisdiction* docket, in which it serves as the court to take evidence but relies on masters to do so. See 28 U.S.C. § 1251.

The federal courts have a staff of some 30,000. The administrative arm is the Administrative Office (AO) of the United States Courts, established in 1939 to take management tasks away from the Department of Justice and internalize them to the judiciary. The AO works on budgets (the federal judiciary's budget is about one quarter of one percent of the nation's), courthouse management for some 500 buildings, security, and staff procedures. Management also is decentralized to the circuits and districts. A second entity within the judiciary is the Federal Judicial Center, established in 1967 and responsible for education and research. See 28 U.S.C. §§ 601 and 620.

The administration of the federal judiciary is under the general supervision of the Judicial Conference of the United States (see 28 U.S.C. § 331), a body of 27 composed of the chief judges of all the circuits and designated district judges and chaired by the Chief Justice. The Judicial Conference has taken on a policymaking role for the Third Branch on issues ranging from cameras in courtrooms to pending legislation on proposed new rights to the need for more judges. In addition, each circuit has its own governing body (a judicial council) and holds regular meetings. 28 U.S.C. § 332.

State court systems are quite varied. Many have a three-tiered structure, with trial courts, intermediate appellate courts to which litigants have rights of appeal, and supreme courts to which access is discretionary. The trial courts of the states are courts of general jurisdiction, in which almost any kind of case can be heard. These general courts may be divided by specialties, such that separate criminal, traffic, surrogate (family and testamentary matters), and juvenile courts exist. Alternatively, some states use a unified court system, with divisions dedicated to special matters. A few states—such as Delaware—still have chancery courts with jurisdiction over cases involving equitable relief. One cannot always tell the level or kind of court from its name. In New York, for example, the general trial court is called the Supreme Court, whereas the highest state court is its Court of Appeals. In California, the Supreme Court is the highest court, and the Superior Court is the trial court. Each state court system has its own administration, sometimes provided by state constitutional provisions. The National Conference of Chief Justices of the State Courts serves as a means of linking the judiciaries of different states. A few other institutions, such as the National Center for State Courts and the Department of Justice's Bureau of Justice Statistics, collect data on the pattern and number of filings in state court systems, which, as noted, vastly outstrips the federal system.

Another set of courts formally recognized by federal law are tribal courts. After the Supreme Court ruled in 1883 that federal courts did not have jurisdiction over crimes committed on Indian lands, the Secretary of the Interior issued regulations establishing "courts of Indian offenses" and staffing those courts with Indian judges. In 1885, Congress passed the Major Crimes Act, now codified as amended at 18 U.S.C. § 1153, which conferred federal jurisdiction over Indians in Indian country for seven specified felonies. In the 1970s, the Supreme Court concluded that Congress had not subjected "non-Indians" committing crimes on tribal lands to tribal criminal jurisdiction. On the civil side, the jurisdictional reach of tribal courts is also tied to the identity of the participants, the nature of the claim, and the geography of tribal lands. In addition, special statutory schemes such as those involving children make provisions for the interaction between state and tribal courts.

More than 400 tribes have received federal recognition, and their courts vary substantially. After the 1934 enactment of the Indian Reorganization Act, the Department of the Interior provided model regulations for tribes to structure their justice systems. Although some tribes retained their traditional tribal courts, many adopted court structures based upon the Interior Department's regulations. These courts became known as "C.F.R. courts," after the sections of the Code of Federal Regulations that set forth court procedures, mechanisms for the selection and removal of judges, and a compilation of "Indian Tribal Offenses." The enactment in 1968 of the Indian Civil Rights Act exerted additional pressure to adopt modes of dispensing justice akin to those used in the states and the federal government rather than relying on customary law. In more recent years, many tribes have made efforts to preserve their own forms of proceedings, and those efforts have also been supported by federal legislation.

As any student of federal/state/tribal court relations will quickly learn, the instances when cases may move between the sets of court systems are varied and complex. In general, once a case is filed in state court, the case proceeds through that system. Unhappy litigants who believe that the state courts have erred on a matter of federal law may request that the United States Supreme Court hear the case, but even if the Court agrees to do so, its review is limited to questions of federal law. See 28 U.S.C. § 1257.

While most state cases can only enter the federal system by way of the United States Supreme Court, a few exceptions exist. For example, under federal habeas corpus jurisdiction, state prisoners who claim that their state court convictions violated the federal Constitution and who have exhausted their state court remedies have limited opportunities to seek relief in federal trial courts. 28 U.S.C. § 2254. Further, cases that are filed in state courts but could have been commenced in federal court may under specified conditions be *removed* prior to trial to the federal courts. See 28 U.S.C. §§ 1441 et seq. No parallel statute for removal from federal to state court exists, but under Supreme Court doctrines of *comity* and *abstention* and certain statutes, federal courts may be barred from hearing certain cases (such as those pertaining to state court criminal proceedings or state tax regimes) that otherwise fall within their jurisdiction. Another mechanism of coordination stems from the constitutional and statutory provisions of "full faith and credit," which, when coupled with the preclusion rules, generally result in the rule that once a case has been litigated in federal or state court, it cannot be relitigated in the other forum. See 28 U.S.C. § 1738.

Another approach involves consolidation and joinder of cases that raise similar issues but are filed in different jurisdictions. Currently, no statutes authorize inter-jurisdictional consolidation between state and federal systems, but settlement practices may function to cross jurisdictional boundaries. Lawyers and judges may work together across state and federal systems to require sharing of discovery as well as to achieve agreements that depend on concluding cases pending in more than one set of courts. Within the federal system, through the Multidistrict Litigation (MDL) Statute, 28 U.S.C. § 1407, cases filed in different federal districts can be consolidated for pre-trial purposes.

B. Administrative Agencies

A large number of federal and state administrative agencies have jurisdiction over disputes arising under specific statutes. Based on their enabling legislation, agencies have the authority to promulgate rules, enforce statutory and regulatory requirements, and determine the rights and liabilities of parties. Thus, in some respects agencies function like executive branch prosecutors, while in others they behave like courts. During the second half of the twentieth century, agencies became increasingly important venues of adjudication. Proceduralists should understand them to be another set of courts, with a specialized focus frequently involving claims against the government. In addition to thinking about whether agency adjudication ought to be assimilated within court systems or have a distinctive character such that administrative law judging will remain a discrete form of adjudication, the concept of agencies themselves merits exploration. The Constitution makes no express provision for agencies. Some commentators conceive of them as a fourth branch of government.

From the country's inception, the Executive Branch has done regulatory and adjudication-like work, such as awarding pensions to veterans and making land grants. During the nineteenth century, more formalized structures were carved out within the Executive; one example is the Bureau of Indian Affairs, created in 1824. Congress created the first formally independent regulatory agency in 1887, when it authorized the Interstate Commerce Commission (ICC) to regulate railroads and other forms of interstate transportation and to prohibit discriminatory ratemaking by interstate railroads and shippers. Persons aggrieved by alleged violations of ICC rules could complain to the ICC, which would then investigate and make findings. The ICC originally had no direct enforcement powers; when the ICC wanted to enforce its regulations and orders, it filed suit in the federal circuit court. After 1910, courts reviewed the ICC's factfinding with a deferential standard. The ICC's report constituted "prima facie evidence" of the facts found.

In 1914, Congress created a second independent regulatory agency, the Federal Trade Commission (FTC), currently detailed at 15 U.S.C. §§ 41–56. Congress thereafter chartered many other administrative agencies, such as the Securities and Exchange Commission (SEC) and the National Labor Relations Board (NLRB), both stemming from the New Deal era, and the Equal Employment Opportunities Commission (EEOC), a product of 1960s civil rights legislation. Administrative agencies exercise control over a great many areas, including the allocation of funds in social welfare programs, the conduct of labor-management relations, environmental protection, and the regulation of securities.

In the late 1930s, policymakers grew concerned about the diversity among agency practices. After World War II, Congress enacted the Administrative Procedure Act (APA), 5 U.S.C. §§ 500 et seq., to regularize some of their functioning. Rulemaking is one of the most important functions that agencies perform, as agencies fill in many interstices of statutes. The APA requires that each agency publish rules and information about its organizational structure. 5 U.S.C. § 552. The Code of Federal Regulations (C.F.R.) includes all such promulgations. Whenever agencies seek to change their rules or to adopt new ones, agencies are obliged to provide notice of their rulemaking and of the substance of a proposed rule 5 U.S.C. § 552. The Federal Register (an almost daily paperback publication) lists all such proposals. The APA requires that interested parties be permitted to submit written statements commenting on proposed rules. Some enabling statutes require agencies to hold oral hearings before promulgating rules.

Agencies generally have investigatory powers; some have authority to conduct searches, issue subpoenas, and hold hearings. Generally speaking, agency investigations must be authorized by law and undertaken for a legitimate purpose. 5 U.S.C. § 555(c). The information sought must not be privileged, and the requests made must be specific and not unduly burdensome. While the Fourth Amendment limits prosecutors' ability to search, the Supreme Court has held that something less than probable cause (as that term is used in the criminal context) is sufficient to grant agencies the authority to search. The Court has approved warrantless searches of welfare recipients' homes by employees of a state agency, warrants authorizing building inspectors to make searches of entire neighborhoods without showing cause to believe any specific building was in violation of a building code, and warrantless entry into the public lobby of a motel for the purpose of serving an administrative subpoena for production of business records. Although the individual or business subpoenaed may challenge the reasonableness of a subpoena, federal district courts must uphold agency subpoenas unless they are "plainly incompetent or irrelevant to any lawful purpose" of the agency. During questioning, however, individuals (but not corporations) may assert their Fifth Amendment privileges.

In addition to drafting and enforcing rules and investigating, agencies adjudicate disputes, and there too, the APA creates a regulatory structure. The APA's rules on adjudication are supplemental. The APA's rules determine procedure unless a specific enabling statute dictates otherwise. The APA's adjudicatory provisions do not apply to informal agency actions, but only to that proportion of agency adjudication which must be "on the record after opportunity for an agency hearing." 5 U.S.C. § 554(a). The APA requires that persons entitled to notice be informed of the time and place of the hearing, the legal authority and jurisdiction under which the hearing is conducted, and the matters to be addressed. 5 U.S.C. § 554(b). The APA also requires that agencies' adjudicatory decisions be based upon information presented at the hearings.

A provision for discovery in the APA comes from the Freedom of Information Act (FOIA), 5 U.S.C. § 552. Added in 1974, FOIA permits members of the public to obtain materials from agencies; FOIA also includes a number of specific exemptions that permit agencies to withhold certain kinds of information. Although FOIA was not designed to provide discovery in agency proceedings, but rather to provide openness in government, FOIA functions in practice to permit some discovery. In addition to the FOIA provisions, some agencies have regulations, analogous to the discovery provisions of the Federal Rules of Civil Procedure, that permit some information exchange prior to adjudication.

Some agency adjudicators are members of an agency's staff, while others are part of a group called "Administrative Law Judges" (ALJs), created by the APA to provide some separation of function within agencies by delineating those who write the rules or investigate individuals from ruling on alleged wrongdoing. 5 U.S.C. § 3105. ALJs are appointed through a merit selection system based upon an examination and, in some cases, experience working within an agency. Another factor is the "veteran's preference," giving points for service in the armed forces. ALJs are assigned to a particular agency but may move to other agencies. ALJs have civil service status and are removable from office only for good cause. 5 U.S.C. § 7521.

More than 1,400 people serve as ALJs. In addition, some agencies also have employees who serve as "hearing officers" or presiding officers, fulfilling judge-like roles but doing so outside the confines of the APA. In other words, within agencies can be two sets of judges, ALJs and another, less formal group, which one scholar termed the "hidden judiciary." Together, these agency judges decide a great many cases. In the late 1990s, the Social Security Administration (SSA) alone dealt with more than 500,000 cases annually, as contrasted with about 260,000 civil filings in the federal courts. The caseload and number of judges of the different federal agencies vary enormously. For example, in 2001, the U.S. Postal Service had one full-time judicial officer, while the Social Security Administration employed 1,100, which is about 80 percent of all federal ALJs.

The APA requires that an ALJ preside at the taking of evidence in any formal adjudicatory hearing not conducted personally by the head of the agency. 5 U.S.C. § 556(b). The APA also requires that ALJs not be assigned to perform duties inconsistent with their judicial functions. ALJs may not adjudicate cases that they have personally investigated or prepared. In addition, ALJs may not have contact, outside of formal proceedings, with the agency staff assigned to investigate or prosecute a case. 5 U.S.C. § 554(d). Formal agency adjudication concludes with the issuance of a written decision. The APA requires that all decisions, whether preliminary or final, include "findings and conclusions, and the reasons or basis therefore, on all the material issues of fact, law or discretion presented on the record." 5 U.S.C. § 557(c).

The APA is not the only test of the adequacy of adjudicatory process of agencies; further, it does not apply to non-federal agencies. The Supreme Court has held that the Constitution provides some limits on agency adjudication, concluding, for example, that when agencies have the power to limit or terminate individuals' entitlements, due process requirements demand that parties receive adequate notice, an impartial decisionmaker, submission of evidence, and decisions keyed to the information presented. Goldberg v. Kelly, 397 U.S. 254 (1970).

Administrative adjudication may be commenced by an individual challenging an administrative ruling with which she or he disagrees. For example, a Social Security recipient may claim that benefits have been wrongly reduced, or a person may file a claim with the Equal Employment Opportunities Commission (EEOC), seeking a finding that he or she has been discriminated against by an employer subject to Title VII. An administrative proceeding may also be commenced by the agency itself, when it seeks to sanction or to require an individual to behave in a particular fashion. For example, the Securities and Exchange Commission may attempt to revoke a broker's license. Each agency's enabling legislation outlines how that agency conducts its adjudicatory business; alongside those rules stand the requirements imposed by the APA and, occasionally, by the federal courts, which may consider whether agency procedures are in compliance with the enabling legislation, with the APA, and with the Constitution.

Federal courts interact with agencies in a variety of ways. One function is to serve as an appellate court for agencies. Under many statutes, dissatisfied claimants can seek federal court review—at either the district or appellate level—of agency adjudication. (The APA is not itself a grant of additional jurisdiction to the federal courts.) An agency's enabling legislation typically designates which court is charged with that task and sets the standard by which the decision is to be judged. For example, federal district or magistrate judges review decisions rendered in social security cases by determining whether the facts found were supported by "substantial evidence." 42 U.S.C. § 405(g). Appeal of the trial level decisions can in turn be had at the circuit level. In contrast, the courts of appeal directly review decisions made by the National Labor Relations Board (NLRB). 45 U.S.C. § 159. When an agency's enabling statute does not specify a standard for review, Section 706 of the APA governs. That section provides that courts may set aside agency actions where the action is: (1) "arbitrary," "capricious," or "an abuse of discretion;" (2) "contrary to a constitutional right;" (3) outside the agency's jurisdiction; (4) made without observing the required procedure; (5) "unsupported by substantial evidence" when there is a formal agency record; or (6) "unwarranted by the facts" to the extent that the facts may be found de novo by the reviewing court. 5 U.S.C. § 706(2). Matters "committed to agency discretion by law" are outside the scope of judicial control. 5 U.S.C. § 701(a).

Federal courts may perform another function in terms of agencies. Under some statutes, agencies need to go to court to enforce orders. Finally, when individuals are dissatisfied with agency decisionmaking but do not have standing to press for direct review through an agency's statute, they may file an affirmative action, arguing the illegality of the procedures by which the decisions are made, of the scope of the decisions, or of the agency's rules themselves. The breadth of judicial review of agency decisionmaking is bounded by a series of doctrines that require courts to be deferential to agencies, but that deference varies depending on the kind of decision that the agency makes. In a few instances, Congress has sought to circumscribe federal court review. Examples include limiting review of the Veterans Administration's benefit rulings (38 U.S.C. § 511(a)) and of those of the Immigration and Naturalization Service (INS). The courts have tended to respond by interpreting such provisions through a due process lens as not completely abrogating a role for the courts.

While holding on to some role after agency decision-making, federal courts rely on the doctrine of *exhaustion of administrative remedies* as a predicate to judicial review. The party seeking review has to exhaust all opportunities for reconsideration provided by the agency. A statutory formulation is the APA's statement that judicial review is available only when agencies have made "final" decisions. 5 U.S.C. § 704. Specific statutes may also impose requirements. For example, individuals challenging a disability determination by the SSA are generally required to seek reconsideration, an oral hearing, and review by the SSA's Appeals Council before turning to a federal court. In addition to such statutory exhaustion requirements, the courts, relying on their inherent powers, sometimes also require exhaustion. This discretionary exhaustion requirement is tempered, somewhat, by exceptions permitting individuals to forego further administrative appeals when the issues involved do not require administrative expertise, when administrative review would be futile because agency positions are not subject to change, when delays are unreasonably long, or when agency remedies are inadequate. But Congress can insist on exhaustion even under those conditions, and it has done so by requiring prisoners challenging conditions of confinement to exhaust administrative remedies, even when they do not provide the monetary relief sought.

During the 1980s and 1990s, Congress revisited issues of agency power, prompted in part by changing conditions and in part to curb agency authority. For example, in 1995 Congress abolished the ICC, transferred some of its ratemaking functions to a newly created entity (the National Surface Transportation Board) and reorganized the Internal Revenue

Service in light of changing taxpayer complaints. In addition, Congress abolished the umbrella institution, the Administrative Conference of the United States, which had functioned to support agencies through study and information exchange. See 5 U.S.C. § 594. Congress also required agencies to promote the use of alternative dispute resolution, through the Administrative Dispute Resolution Act of 1996, 5 U.S.C. §§ 571 et seq., discussed below. Congress has also relied on, and the Supreme Court has approved, the use of agencies for expanded roles in adjudication and negotiation of disputes. For example, agency judges gained authority to hear related claims when disputes arose under the Commodities Futures Trading Act, and the Supreme Court approved that use despite arguments that agency adjudication was invading the role of life-tenured judges under Article III. Moreover, using its own administrative voice, the federal judiciary has recommended transferring certain types of statutory claims to agency-based adjudicators.

Like the federal government, the states have also increased their reliance upon agencies. In California, statutes list some sixty-five boards, commissions, and departments as state agencies, each with their own jurisdiction and responsibilities. Similarly, in New York, agency regulations, governing matters from banking to housing to transportation, have resulted in dozens of volumes of the New York Code of Rules and Regulations. A national concern for uniformity and regularity in agency procedures prompted the National Conference of Commissioners on Uniform State Laws to create, in 1946, a nonbinding Model State Administrative Procedures Act (Model Act). Model State Administrative Procedures Act, 15 U.L.A. (1981). Revised in 1961 and in 1981, the Model Act, like the federal APA, aims to establish consistency in agency procedures by addressing rulemaking, adjudication, freedom of information, and judicial review. By 1986, thirty states had passed legislation based upon the Model Act. Other states, such as California, have their own administrative procedure statutes. As in the federal system, California's APA is limited in scope, applying only to some agencies and leaving others to make their own procedural rules.

C. Alternative Dispute Resolution

Civil, criminal, and administrative processes, all publicly sponsored methods of responding to disputes, are premised upon a triadic structure: disputants seek decisionmaking by a third party who acts in a relatively formal manner according to preexisting rules and who renders judgment. The third-party decisionmaker is empowered by the state, acts on behalf of the state, and has the coercive authority of the state available to enforce the judgments made. The decisionmaker's behavior is circumscribed by a series of public norms delineating what the third party may do, and the decisionmaker's judgments are either made in public or reported to the public.

In recent decades, some have grown uneasy with this structure. Changes in industries, technology (such as computers, photocopying), and the legal profession, plus the creation of new causes of action ranging from consumer to environmental to civil rights, prompted some to complain that access to courts was too easy, others to bemoan the costs of litigation, and still others to decry its combative qualities. Those critiques, founded on very different ideologies and representing a range of political values, came together under a self-conscious movement—*Alternative Dispute Resolution* (ADR).

In both civil and criminal contexts, many enthusiasts argue that ADR offers several advantages making it more desirable than adjudication. First, some commentators see ADR as enhancing party participation and control. Second, because of that participation, some claim that ADR yields better outcomes than does adjudication. Third, by diverting disputants away from adjudication, some believe that ADR provides a less expensive, and sometimes speedier, decisionmaking procedure.

In contrast, critics of ADR insist that the informality may provide too little by way of remedy or sanction and too much power to decisionmakers, whose judgments are shielded from public scrutiny. Enthusiasm and concern ought to rely in part on empirical understandings of ADR and of adjudication. Although many claims of speedy and inexpensive process are made, less evidence is available than one would hope. But a small and growing body of studies seeks to understand the costs and benefits, measured not only in terms of speed and expenses to courts and parties but also in terms of quality of process and outcome.

ADR is an umbrella term that encompasses a range of processes (including negotiation, mediation, and arbitration) and of places. Negotiation is a process by which disputants conclude their conflict through agreement. Negotiation is often praised for permitting the parties to set the terms of their own remedies and thereby to exercise control over the outcome. Parties may negotiate directly or through representatives (such as lawyers). While informal, negotiation is norm-bounded. The parties act under a set of social descriptions of appropriate behavior and invoke rules to determine their application to the facts at hand. Further, negotiations may range from congenial, mutually-engaged exchanges to those of a more adversarial character. Like adjudication, negotiation takes place in a social context of economic and political inequality and offers limited means by which to correct for such imbalance.

Mediation introduces a third party, sometimes selected by the disputants, to enter negotiations to facilitate a mutually satisfactory outcome. The mediator lacks authority to impose a solution. Rather, the aspiration is that the mediator's "good offices" will permit the parties to gain insight into how they can achieve compromise. Mediation techniques vary; some mediators aspire to *facilitate* while others see their role as *evaluative*. Some mediators meet separately with both sides (*caucusing*) and then bring the parties together, while others engage in what might be termed shuttle diplomacy. Some mediators are trained, often in professions other than law. Mediations can be voluntarily arranged by disputants or required by court-based programs, in which case lawyers and judges commonly fill the function of mediators, engaging in a range of styles and sometimes working in programs with titles such as early neutral evaluation or settlement days.

In arbitration, a third party is also employed (again either chosen by the disputants or assigned by the courts), but in contrast to mediation, that third party has the authority to impose an outcome. Arbitration can be binding or nonbinding. Arbitration is also distinguished from adjudication in that the hearings are often more informal than court proceedings, arbitrators are not required to explain how their rulings accord with prior principles, and arbitrators' decisions do not become part of a formal body of precedential authority. As a consequence, both the sources of decisions and the outcomes may be at variance with what adjudication might have produced.

As indicated, ADR can be court-based, in that courts can require disputants to engage in ADR as a predicate to litigation. ADR can also be court-enforced, in that courts can decline to adjudicate disputes because of disputants' agreements to forego adjudication. Public dispute resolution systems thus play an important role in either promoting or limiting private-based resolution and in shaping its own processes to incorporate alternatives.

Consider the question of enforcing contracts to arbitrate. During the nineteenth century, courts were skeptical of arbitration and refused to cede their jurisdiction by declining to enforce private contracts that required arbitration in lieu of adjudication. In 1925, however, Congress enacted the United States Arbitration Act, 9 U.S.C. §§ 1–14 (now the Federal Arbitration Act or the FAA), which overturned the common law view that private agreements to arbitrate, made before disputes arose, were unenforceable. The prior rule—that parties' consent could not deprive a court of jurisdiction—gave way to the conception that parties' mutual desires to seek decisionmaking elsewhere would be enforceable, even after one party reneged and sought adjudication.

In the 1980s and thereafter, the Court read the FAA broadly, making it a means of removing cases to federal court and staying state proceedings and reading the FAA legislation to apply to a range of state-based claims, including employment discrimination. Further, while the Court had during the 1950s read other federal statutes (such as securities regulations) as permitting enforcement of arbitration agreements only after disputes arose, by the 1980s the Court revised its interpretation of several such statutes and enforced arbitration clauses, as long as arbitration provided a means effective to vindicate the federal statutory rights.

Once an arbitrator has ruled, an unhappy disputant has two principal means by which to challenge an award in court. A first is to argue either that the arbitrator exceeded his or her authority under the contract or that procedural defects (such as bias) undermined the validity of the award. See, e.g. Federal Arbitration Act, 9 U.S.C. § 10. A second is to attack the decision on the merits as wrong. But because both state and federal law are protective of arbitration, the first route—procedural or structural irregularity—is more often countenanced than the second, which in essence would provide for appellate review of arbitrators' judgments.

On the federal side, one route to argue procedural inadequacy has been marked. Because the Supreme Court has said that arbitration of federal statutory rights is only required if those rights enable a disputant to vindicate the particular legal right at stake, the claim can be made—before an arbitration has occurred—that a specific arbitration process is not an effective means of doing so, for example because it costs more than or offers less than would court-based process. See, e.g., Green Tree Financial Corp. v. Randolph, 531 U.S. 79 (2000). A subsidiary issue is who has the burden of making that showing, and *Green Tree* responded by placing the obligation on the party objecting to arbitration. Another issue is how much arbitration processes have to mirror court processes. Illustrative debates here, currently in lower courts, address whether arbitration clauses are unenforceable because aggregate processes, such as class actions, are not available.

The law on the interaction between arbitration and adjudication is relatively recent. As Supreme Court decisions enforcing arbitration clauses mount, more manufacturers and suppliers are inserting such clauses into form contracts relating to goods and services such as cellular phones, credit cards, and money market funds. If courts require arbitration to mimic adjudication as a predicate to enforcing such contracts, then parties proposing arbitration have incentives to make their programs richer with procedural opportunities. But disputants opposed to using arbitration clauses need both to know about the ability to contest the provisions and to have the resources to do so. Further, to the extent the justification for using these clauses is their relative informality vis a vis courts, judges appear reluctant to insist on exacting measures of equivalency and have been willing to find that many processes permit "effective vindication" of statutory rights.

A second kind of attack on arbitration is mounted after the conclusion of an arbitration and goes to the outcome, rather than the process. The federal arbitration statute is protective of awards, as are parallel state provisions. In other words, arbitration awards have a form of finality—no appellate review—that is not common in contemporary courts other than small claims courts. Illustrative is Moncharsh v. Heily & Blase, 10 Cal. Rptr. 2d 183 (1992). There, the California Supreme Court declined to review the arbitrator's award despite claims that the award appeared erroneous on its face and would cause substantial injustice. Some argued further that, given California's statutory commitment to arbitration, judicially-confirmed arbitration awards should have the same force and effect as civil judgments, which is to say that they would be res judicata, and could also be used for non-mutual collateral estoppel. That view was rejected in Vandenberg v. Superior Court, 21 Cal. 4th 815 (1999). In other words, although appellate review of arbitration awards is not available, arbitration awards have less subsequent effect, in that they cannot serve as formal precedent nor can they preclude subsequent court-based decisionmaking.

An issue implicit in the discussion above is the relationship between federal and state law. The Supreme Court has read federal statutes to *preempt* state law—to displace the authority of state courts and legislatures over these issues of contract and access to courts. For example, in one case, a man sought to challenge his employer as violating state anti-discrimination statutes but, the Court held, because he had agreed in his employment contract to mandatory arbitration of all claims, he could not go to state court. Circuit City Stores v. St. Clair Adams, 532 U.S. 105 (2001). Some commentators object to such "federalization" of arbitration policy. Yet state law remains relevant (in both state and federal courts) because it is often the basis for interpreting the words of contracts, and some courts have declined to enforce arbitration on the grounds of a lack of clarity of a particular clause or a lack of mutuality of bargaining.

In addition to the issues of enforcing and interpreting contracts requiring ADR, another question is the role arbitration and other ADR processes play within courts themselves. Increasingly, courts write ADR into their own rules and make it an integral part of civil processing. State and federal systems have detailed rules requiring various kinds of ADR, and Congress has been supportive of that effort, first in 1990 with the Civil Justice Reform Act, encouraging such programs, and then in 1998, with the Alternative Dispute Resolution Act, 28 U.S.C. § 651 et seq., requiring the district courts to authorize the use of alternative dispute resolution, to implement their own ADR programs, and to provide litigants with at least one ADR method to consider.

Professional organizations of dispute resolution providers also promote its use. For example, the American Arbitration Association trains professionals and provides referral services. When ADR occurs as a result of a contract, the contract may detail what providers and what process to use and what costs will be imposed. As such arbitration clauses make their way into a range of consumer contracts, issues of cost, access, and enforceability arise as described above. Like the litigation system, some disputants also have the capacity to shop ADR systems, not only by providing them for their employees or for purchasers of their products but also by selecting individuals, on a case-by-case basis, to serve as judges. Programs such as "rent-a-judge" and consortiums of providers market such services to those able to afford to do so.

Both the processes (adjudication, negotiation, mediation, and arbitration) and the venues (public and private dispute resolution) are therefore deeply intermeshed, and changes in one affect the others. Moreover, parties often engage in negotiations while simultaneously pursuing adjudication.

Further, role delineations are not always sharp. Today, judges often attempt to mediate, and some arbitrators may develop informal precedents that function quite like formal adjudication. Indeed, the distinctions have diminished as courts embrace ADR and as ADR becomes more structured. For example, *court-annexed arbitration,* run by courts, is sometimes required as a precedent to trial. Rather than parties selecting arbitrators, courts appoint lawyers to act as arbitrators and to render decisions after hearings at which parties present their views. In these proceedings, the rules are set by the courts, not agreed upon by the parties. Court-annexed arbitrations closely resemble less formal trials at which, in lieu of judge or jury, lawyers or other court officials reach decisions. In addition, while adjudication is often described as a win/lose activity, decisions by juries and judges often entail compromises. Moreover, given that a substantial percentage of cases in which adjudication has been sought conclude without adjudication (by settlement or voluntary withdrawal of litigation), some object to the characterization of adjudication as the norm and the other processes as the "alternatives." Some have therefore dropped the "alternative" from ADR and refer instead to "Dispute Resolution" or DR; what we might call procedural-ists, they term "dispute resolution designers."

Exploration of the use of ADR on the criminal side also has occurred, but here public funding is a key aspect. One effort, called "Neighborhood Justice Centers" (NJC), began in 1977 with federal grants for three programs in Atlanta, Kansas City, and Los Angeles to help settle disagreements before cases were filed. These centers were intended to enable individuals, typically in ongoing relationships and referred by police or social services, to resolve disputes without intervention by the justice system. Federal funding declined soon thereafter, but some programs continued under the auspices of charities and local governments.

Another kind of criminal ADR occurs after an arrest has been made or charges are filed or pending. In many courts, discretionary "pretrial diversion" programs exist to halt the pending prosecution for a period of time, and in some instances, to abort the proceedings in their entirety. For example, for individuals charged with substance abuse, charges may be suspended in exchange for an agreement to participate in a detoxification or rehabilitation program. In the 1990s, some of those efforts became known as "therapeutic justice" and self-consciously used judges in conjunction with social workers to shift behavior through a structured program of having offenders report regularly to specific judges. After defendants successfully complete such programs, their charges may be dismissed or sanctions reduced. In other cases, such as fraud or petty theft, the prosecutor may defer filing charges and refer the parties to mediation. If restitution is made and both parties agree to forego further legal action, the prosecutor takes no further action.

Guidelines for such diversion programs typically limit them to misdemeanor offenses such as assault, fraud, vandalism, domestic violence, and some kinds of substance abuse. Defendants' criminal record, history of violent crime, youth, employment status, and desire to forestall a criminal conviction are taken into consideration in weighing whether diversion is appropriate. Also in the 1990s, questions emerged about the wisdom of using such programs for domestic violence. In contrast to efforts at informal conciliation among disputants, several localities passed mandatory prosecution statutes, prohibiting police and prosecutors from dropping or deferring criminal prosecutions of allegations of violence.

D. International Tribunals

The power of courts is tied to the power of the government of which they are a part. Governments in turn have long measured their authority by reference to the physical boundaries over which they have control. As technology and transportation reduce the import of geographical borders, new questions are posed for courts. The pressures for international, transnational, and multi-national responses, based in both public courts and private contracts, stem from all arenas (from family life and commercial transactions to organized crime and war) and raise many conceptual problems about the role of national courts and the place of international dispute resolution mechanisms.

One set of questions relates to the reach of national courts, seeking to adjudicate events involving persons or activities beyond their borders. Another set of issues addresses the role of international courts and the reach of their jurisdiction, sometimes limited only to nations that consent to a specific instance and otherwise conceived to be more broad-ranging. Another concern relates to the interaction between national, subnational, and international adjudication. As judicial bodies of varying kinds have proliferated during the later part of the twentieth century, the import of such problems for both domestic and international tribunals has similarly grown.

In some instances, when individuals violate a nation's law but are not physically within that country's boundaries, national courts claim jurisdiction by seizing the person of the defendant—either by requesting that, pursuant to a treaty, another country extradite that person or by forcibly bringing that person to the jurisdiction for trial. In other instances, the injuries occur beyond that country's boundaries. For example, beginning in 1789 with the First Judiciary Act, Congress has given federal courts jurisdiction over tort claims filed by aliens alleging a "violation of the law of nations." Cases have been filed under this statute challenging torture and property seizure that occurred in countries other than the United States. See 28 U.S.C. § 1350.

International tribunals may also respond and, some argue, are especially important to deploy in cases when jurisdiction beyond the nation-state is sought to be exercised. For example, in 1948, the Charter of the United Nations (UN) established the International Court of Justice (the ICJ) which sits in the Hague, Netherlands. All state members of the UN are subject to the ICJ's jurisdiction, although in some instances, member states decline to participate. For example, in the 1980s the United States declined to do so when Nicaragua sought redress for this country's alleged involvement in its civil war; the ICJ, however, ruled on the merits that the United States had violated international customary law by intervening. In the 1970s, the court had but a few cases on its docket. By the 1990s, its docket grew to about ten cases a year and, as of 2000, it had twenty-three cases before it.

In addition to the ICJ, the UN also has many conventions addressed to specific issues (such as racism, discrimination against women, and the rights of children), and these conventions often create expert bodies or committees that receive information from countries and review their work in a quasi-adjudicative capacity. Some have optional protocols permitting individuals to bring complaints, although the remedies provided may be advisory rather than binding. Further, the UN has set up special tribunals to deal with individual claims arising out of events such as the Gulf War and the 1981 Iranian revolution.

More recently, proposals have sought to establish courts with jurisdiction to provide transnational responses to all "crimes against humanity," such as genocide. After World War II, ad hoc tribunals (the Nuremberg and Tokyo Tribunals) were constituted. In the 1990s, under the auspices of the United Nations, special courts were convened to deal with prosecutions arising in Rwanda and the Former Territories of Yugoslavia. Their mandates rely on the crimes detailed in the Geneva Protocols of 1949 and the 1977 Additional Protocols. In 1999, many countries joined in the Rome Treaty for an International Criminal Court (ICC) to establish a permanent prosecutorial and adjudicatory body that would have the power to adjudicate crimes against humanity, as specified by that Treaty. That proposal has engendered substantial controversy about which persons would be called to account for what forms of behavior. Since the Rome Treaty has been ratified by more than a requisite sixty countries (although not by the United States), the ICC entered into force on July 1, 2002. The International Criminal Court is expected to supplement many existing institutions and to be used in lieu of ad hoc responses to specific conflicts.

The World Trade Organization (WTO) is yet another source of courts. Its 1995 initiating agreement includes a "dispute settlement understanding" that created a Dispute Panel and Appellate Body. Private traders and investors have the power, pursuant to their respective domestic laws, to request that their governments take action against unreasonable foreign trade measures. Access to the processes of the Global Agreement on Tariffs and Trade (GATT) and of the WTO does not always require exhausting local remedies, and the speed of resolution and volume of cases has grown considerably. As of 1999, there were about 100 cases in the WTO system.

In addition to proceedings under specific UN Conventions and the WTO processes, regional federations have also created courts with a jurisdictional span broader than that of a single nation-state. The European Union, comprised of 15 states, and the Council of Europe (41 states) have two such courts: the European Courts of Justice (both trial and appellate), sitting in Luxembourg, and a specialized court, the European Court of Human Rights, sitting in Strasbourg, France. The latter court deals with claims by individuals seeking review of decisions from their own domestic courts alleged to be in contravention of the European Convention on Human Rights.

As is true domestically, international agreements often include alternative dispute resolution provisions. Sometimes private international organizations or commercial entities contract to use such processes; nation-states may also incorporate these dispute resolution mechanisms in their treaties. For example, the International Olympic Committee prompted the creation of the Court of Arbitration for Sport with 150 arbitrators, sitting for four-year terms and dealing with individual parties' disputes and sports federation discipline, and providing advisory opinions. The North American Free Trade Agreement (NAFTA) and many bilateral investment treaties also permit individuals to pursue claims through the United Nations Commission for International Trade Law (UNCITRAL) and the International Center for the Settlement of Investment Disputes (ICSID). All of these systems have to face questions about enforceability of their judgments in case of noncompliance, which in turn often relate to whether "local law" recognizes the authority of such contracts and defers to such decisionmakers.

All multi-national courts and dispute resolution processes have the challenge of developing forms of processing that resolve differences among competing national paradigms. The questions that are outlined in this volume—from party structure to the power of decisionmakers, from the mode of information exchange to the standards of proof—must be faced as each dispute resolution system comes into being.

VI. THE PARTICIPANTS

Who litigates? Who are the lawyers and judges? Who sits on juries? During the past few decades, questions of identity and of resources have become regular aspects of discussions about legal processes. From perspectives ranging from critical theory to law and economics, attention has turned to the users of legal systems to understand their diverse capacities, interests, and incentives.

Below, I provide an overview of court-sponsored efforts aimed at learning about whether individuals' experiences of the justice system vary depending on the gender, race, religion, or ethnicity of the respondents. After describing some of what we have learned (and what we do not know) about those who participate in legal processes, I turn to three central institutional players—juries, judges, and lawyers. Both jurors and judges hold the power of judgment, making important a fuller understanding of how people become jurors and judges and of the breadth and limits of their authority. This chapter closes with discussion of the right to counsel, of the importance of lawyers, and of the costs of lawyering. In this discussion of access and equipage, I detail some of the mechanisms for paying lawyers through state-funded subsidies, for fee-shifting and fee-sharing among litigants, and for buying legal services in the private market.

A. Broadening Participatory Rights: Gender, Race, Ethnicity and the Courts

Although "equality under law" has long been stated as an ideal, the legal and judicial professions were, until the twentieth century, functionally closed to individuals on the bases of race, gender, religion, and ethnicity. Under English law for example, only "persons" could qualify for the bar and the word "persons" was interpreted as not including women. In addition, the rights of initiation and of participation in legal processes were not always held by women of all colors and by men of color. Only during the last two hundred years have all persons gained juridical capacity—to file lawsuits, to testify, and to serve as judges and as jurors.

As these barriers were slowly dissolved, the individuals who challenged them often formed specialized associations to help sustain them in their efforts. In 1899, for example, a few women started the National Association of Women Lawyers; in 1925, a group of African–American lawyers began the National Bar Association to advance civil rights. In conjunction with substantive laws recognizing all persons as equal rightsholders, the demographics of the profession began to shift.

By the 1960s and 1970s, as women litigated about their rights, they found that some of the pain of discrimination came from the very places to which they brought claims: the courts. In an effort to educate judges about their assumptions regarding the roles of women and men, the Legal Defense and Education Fund of the National Organization of Women founded the "National Judicial Education Program" (NJEP), which, in cooperation with the National Association of Women Judges (an organization begun in the late 1970s), focused on what is now termed "gender bias" in the courts. A principal mechanism for responding became the creation of Gender Bias Task Forces to document problems jurisdiction by jurisdiction and to generate focused educational programs and specific reforms.

New Jersey led the way in 1982 when its state Chief Justice, Robert N. Wilentz, created the first such task force. New Jersey again was first, in 1985, when it created the first task force addressing "minority concerns," and again, in 1997, when Chief Justice Deborah Poritz created the Task Force on Gay and Lesbian Issues. These projects addressed an array of topics, including the demographics of courthouses, the application of substantive legal doctrine, courtroom interactions, and the role of the court as employer. By 1988, the Chief Justices of all the state courts had adopted a resolution calling for study of gender, racial, and ethnic bias; a few years later, they called for implementation of reforms. By the end of the 1990s, task force activity officially commissioned by judiciaries existed in more than half the states.

From 1982 until 1990, task forces on gender, race, and ethnic bias in the courts were exclusively an artifact of state courts. The federal courts (either acting circuit by circuit or as a whole by action of the Judicial Conference of the United

States) neither took the lead nor followed. However, beginning in 1990, the federal courts began to take up the question. In 1992, the Ninth Circuit became the first within the federal system to issue a report on the effects of gender. In the same year, the Judicial Conference of the United States called for studies of gender bias. Soon thereafter, federal legislation also encouraged such studies, and work began in the District of Columbia's federal courts, as well as those of the First, Second, Eighth, Tenth, and Eleventh Circuits.

The initial phase of activity enjoyed widespread support but, by the mid–1990s, opposition emerged. A group of federal judges refused to provide information, by gender and race, on the persons chosen as law clerks. Judges enlisted a few members of Congress to investigate task forces, attacked as causing "faction" in civil society and undermining judicial independence; they tried to block funding. Such efforts chilled the activities but did not quell them, and about half the circuits have published reports addressing the effects of gender, race, religion, and ethnicity on their processes.

Before considering what those reports discussed, a snapshot of the participants is in order. As of 2000, women of all colors were about half of the students entering law school. Women were about 20 percent of the tenured professors, about 30 percent of practicing private lawyers, under 15 percent of partners, about 40 percent of legal aid lawyers and public defenders, and about 15–20 percent of the judges in the state and federal systems. People of color were 20 percent of those who entered law school classes, 11 percent of tenured faculty, 8 percent of practicing lawyers, 3 percent of partners, and 12 percent of judges. Analyses that track cohorts note that, while women have graduated from law schools in significant percentages for about three decades, they are not represented at the same number in an array of positions. The number of people within a given "pool" of eligible candidates has proven not to be the only variable in gaining promotions, seniority, and authority. The passage of time has not had as much impact as some had hoped.

According to data from the Alliance for Justice in 2000, about 72 percent of the active federal district and circuit judges (some 850 in number) were white. Disaggregation is useful, as the percentages of women and men of all colors are not evenly distributed. For example, in 2000, the Court of Appeals for the Fourth Circuit (an area of the South with a high percentage of African–Americans in its population) gained its first African–American jurist. Looking at the administrative judiciary, a recent survey reports that 88 percent (or 1,096) of the 1,245 federal administrative law judges were men, of whom 91 percent were white. Of the 149 women administrative law judges, 85 percent were white. Turning to the state courts, women were 23 percent of state appellate judiciaries. Of 50 Chief Justices, 15 (30 percent) were women. The numbers and percentages of judges of color on state benches vary dramatically by states. Estimates are that about ten percent of state judges are of color.

Of course, judges are a small percentage of those who work in courts. In the federal system, about 2,000 judges (statutory and constitutional) are joined by about 30,000 other personnel. The American Bar Association (ABA), with several projects on minorities in the professions, has gathered information about who works in courts. In terms of diversity for judicial clerkships, for example, the ABA reported that since 1972, less than two percent of the 428 people who had served as Supreme Court law clerks were African American. From other databases, we know that some 98 percent of judicial secretaries are women. Juries are, in contrast to the judiciary, a more demographically diverse institution. The Ninth Circuit's task forces learned that women were 50 percent of the grand juries. The D.C. task force reported that women served on petit juries in larger numbers; a six-month sample found women were more than 60 percent of the seated jurors.

Turn now some of the findings of the reports on gender, race, and ethnicity. Many detail problems of bias as experienced by litigants, lawyers, court staff, and sometimes by judges themselves. More than twenty reports document that women as witnesses face special hurdles: their credibility is readily questioned, their claims of injury undervalued. In general, members of gender and racial minorities report that sometimes, court-based interactions, and particularly those off the record, are affected by race, ethnicity, and gender bias, and that on occasion, employment opportunities for lawyers and staff are limited by these forms of bias. In contrast, members of majorities describe few or no problems.

After accumulating such data, task forces offered assessments. The conclusions of the Report of the New York Task Force on Women in the Courts, published in 1986, are illustrative of state court reports: "Gender bias against women . . . is a pervasive problem with grave consequences. . . . Cultural stereotypes of women's role in marriage and in society daily distort courts' application of substantive law. Women uniquely disproportionately, and with unacceptable frequency, must endure a climate of condescension, indifference and hostility." Other states' reports echoed this theme: "[W]omen are treated differently from men in the justice system and, because of it, many suffer from unfairness, embarrassment, emotional pain, professional deprivation, and economic hardship." Task forces on racial and ethnic bias come to parallel conclusions: "[T]he perception [is] that minorities are stripped of their human dignity, their individuality and their identity in their encounters with the court system." "[T]here is evidence that bias does occur with disturbing frequency at every level of the legal profession and court system."

All of the reports included proposals for reform. When issued, most reports were generally greeted with efforts to implement them, although the scope, degree, and energy has varied substantially from jurisdiction to jurisdiction. In general, through such work, bias became a topic of judicial conferences, of lawyer meetings, and of private discussions. Sexual harassment policies have been developed, canons of ethics rewritten, legislation enacted, and training programs created to respond to specific problems, such as those faced by victims of home-based violence. Further, the concerns evidenced in such reports are not limited to the domestic context. For example, the treaty creating the proposed new International Criminal Court (ICC) requires that efforts be made by member states to ensure that the court's prosecutors and judges include women and men. The ICC's rules also require that services be provided specifically for victims of sexual assaults.

Move from experiences within courts to the resources provided to courts, and start with compensation for judges. In the federal system, as of 2000, the salaries ranged from around $186,000 for the Chief Justice to $145,000 for district judges; the statutorily-appointed magistrate and bankruptcy judges receive $133,492, 92 percent of the district court judges' salaries. State court salaries are surveyed periodically by the National Center for State Courts. As of 2000, justices' salaries on state high courts ranged from a low of about $84,000 in Montana to a high of $153,000 in Illinois. Salaries of trial judges ranged from a low of $77,000 (again in Montana) to a high of $137,000 in New York. Administrative judges usually earn somewhat less, often tied to civil service grades.

Resources in other forms—from court houses and law clerks to travel budgets, computers, health plans, and pensions—affect daily life, the value of compensation packages, and the attractiveness of work in the public sector. Indeed, a longstanding complaint from federal judges has been inadequate compensation, with reference made to the salaries of lawyers working for large law firms. Some federal judges have also pursued these concerns through litigation. In several lawsuits, they have argued that congressional alterations of cost-of-living adjustments and Social Security taxes violated Article III's guarantee against salary diminution. Such problems are not limited to the domestic setting. The Canadian Supreme Court ruled that separation of powers principles mandate that judicial salaries be set through an independent body, empowered to provide increases.

Turning to private providers of judicial services, their fees vary widely. When those individuals are hired from major law firms or are themselves former judges, they can command rates that are higher than judicial salaries, with hourly fees of more than $300. As for private practitioners, in the late 1990s, male lawyers had an annual median salary of $70,000; female lawyers earned $50,000. In contrast, some partners at major commercial firms earned hundreds of thousands of dollars each year.

Learning about who uses the courts, as contrasted with who works within them, is more difficult. Demographics of litigants are difficult to obtain. Data are kept for criminal defendants, in part because facilities for detention are sex-segregated and in part because of concern about the correlation between race and detention. In 1997, about 85 percent of the 5.7 million people on probation, in jail or prison, or on parole were men. About 38 percent were persons of color. While incarceration rates of non-whites have long been disproportionate to their percentages in the population at large, the skew has worsened recently, with African Americans incarcerated at a rate eight times greater and Hispanics incarcerated at a rate three times greater than European–Americans. Thus far, the Supreme Court has declined to permit challenges to systemic selective prosecution or to race-influenced sentencing. However, during the late 1990s, public attention focused on the problem of "racial profiling" (that law enforcement was selective, based on the perceived race, sex, ethnicity, and age of a person and where a person was) and returned to the problem of police brutality.

In general, less is known about the demographics of civil litigants. Specialized surveys provide some information. For example, about two-thirds of consumers filing for bankruptcy in the early 1990s were white; about 75 percent were either women filing singly or with their spouses. While it is difficult to identify with specificity persons who file cases, it is easier to identify institutional participants and the kinds of cases that courts hear. The single most important litigant in federal courts is the government. The United States government has been a participant (as either plaintiff or defendant) in about 23 percent of the cases in the last five years, with the number steadily increasing. Over the same period, about 20 percent of the cases were predicated on diversity jurisdiction, often involving tort or contract cases in which individuals or corporations come from different states.

B. The Role of Juries

Many countries rely on lay judges, making rulings as individuals, in small groups, or by joining on panels with professional judges. But juries in the United States have an unusually high profile, meriting specific attention to the legal parameters of their role. Before turning to an overview of the jury system, however, readers should be reminded that the use of juries in both civil and criminal proceedings is relatively rare because trials themselves are, as discussed earlier, rare events. Recall that in the federal system, fewer than 3 percent of the civil filings and eight percent of the criminal filings conclude with a trial. Moreover, trial rates have declined steadily, down from under 20 percent in the 1940s, to 12 percent in the 1970s, to the current numbers. In the 1920s, a law review article focused on the "Vanishing Jury," and today a major project of the American Bar Association's Section on Litigation is the "Vanishing Trial."

But juries are nonetheless central because debates about their use, size, composition, and place in United States law have spanned the country's history. Further, for many non-lawyers, a call to jury service is their connection to the legal system. Hence, an appreciation for the constitutional parameters and conflicts about jury deployment, in addition the description of the rules framing juries, as outlined in Chapter I, is required for those literate in American procedure.

The jury system has its roots in the English common law and remains one of the most distinctive features of Anglo–American jurisprudence. In the late Middle Ages and Renaissance, the jury was comprised of people familiar with the events in question, and until the nineteenth century, jurors were those who came to cases with prior information about disputes. They were witnesses. Today those who sit in judgment are required not to have any prior familiarity with the case.

The jury is constitutionally enshrined by two provisions that articulate rights to jury trials, the Sixth and Seventh Amendments. On the criminal side, the Sixth Amendment provides that: "In all criminal prosecutions, the accused shall enjoy the right to a speedy and public trial, by an impartial jury of the State and district wherein the crime shall have been committed. . . ." The United States Supreme Court, under its doctrine of selective incorporation, has held that the Fourteenth Amendment makes the Sixth Amendment jury trial guarantee applicable to the states. Duncan v. Louisiana, 391 U.S. 145 (1968). One question is: To what categories of cases does the jury right apply? The Court has required jury trials only in non-petty offenses with a jail term of six months or more and not in trials of juveniles.

A second question concerns the form the criminal jury must take. Must the jury be comprised of twelve individuals? The Court has held that six-person juries in state criminal cases are permissible, but that five-person juries are not. Compare Williams v. Florida, 399 U.S. 78 (1970) with Ballew v. Georgia, 435 U.S. 223 (1978). The Court has also held that in state criminal trials unanimous verdicts are not required unless there is a jury of six people instead of twelve. Burch v. Louisiana, 441 U.S. 130 (1979); Williams v. Florida, 399 U.S. 78 (1970). The Federal Rules of Criminal Procedure provide for trial by twelve jurors absent parties' stipulations. Fed. R. Crim. P. 23(b). The Rules also require unanimity in federal criminal trials. Fed. R. Crim. P. 31. But a court may also accept a verdict from a jury of eleven if the court finds good cause to excuse a juror. The Court's line-drawing in this area has been the subject of criticism from social scientists, distressed at the uses (or abuses) of research on small group decisionmaking.

The Constitution also addresses the right to a jury trial in civil cases. The Seventh Amendment provides that:

> In suits at common law, where the value in controversy shall exceed twenty dollars, the right of trial by jury shall be preserved, and no fact tried by a jury shall be otherwise reexamined in any court of the United States, than according to the rules of the common law.

On the civil side, the size of the jury has also shrunk. In the 1980s, federal district courts shifted to a smaller civil jury while the relevant federal rule (Fed. R. Civ. P. 48) still presumed a twelve person jury. District court judges became committed to being able to conclude a trial even if some jurors dropped out. However, criticism of the current practice remains—in part because of research demonstrating that group size matters, in part because the question of size intersects with that of the diversity of the members selected, and in part because jury service has been shown to engender positive views of the legal system.

The Seventh Amendment does not, according to the Supreme Court, govern the right to civil jury trials in the states. (The grand jury provisions of the Fifth Amendment have also not been applied to the states.) Thus, the question of a right to a jury trial in a civil action in state court is governed by state constitutional provisions and statutes.

The Seventh Amendment also does not require a comprehensive right to a jury trial. Rather, the right to a civil jury is "preserved" only in a subset of cases. Interpreting the meaning of this guarantee has prompted sustained debate, with some arguing that what is preserved is what English common law recognized as cases for jury decisions, others claiming that it required incorporation of state-based common law practices, and yet others reading the Amendment as giving Congress a good deal of discretion over when juries can be authorized to render verdicts in the federal system.

Once one decides that the right to a jury trial attaches in a particular case or for a particular element of a crime, the next question is how to select the jury. First, citizens eligible for jury service must be identified. This list of eligible citizens is called the *jury pool*. The first Judiciary Act in 1789 relied on state definitions of qualifications for jurors, and many states required not only voting eligibility but also taxpaying, property holding, and evidence of good character. Some statutes expressly excluded people of color and most excluded all white women. Even where these barriers were eliminated, local authorities were free to choose a wide variety of methods, some of which built on networks of acquaintance. In 1972, in the context of the Sixth Amendment right to an impartial jury trial, the Supreme Court held that a cross-section of the community must be included in the pool from which jurors are selected. Peters v. Kiff, 407 U.S. 493 (1972).

From the jury pool, the court must select the *venire*, or the group of people who will be summoned for jury service at a particular time. For how selection of the venire is now done in the federal system, see 28 U.S.C. §§ 1861 et seq.

Typically, voter registration lists or lists of those actually voting in a given election are put into a master jury wheel and the venire is randomly selected from such lists. 28 U.S.C. § 1863 also provides for voter lists to be supplemented by other lists in order to meet Section 1861's goal that a jury venire include a "fair cross section of the community." Some case law suggests that supplementation is infrequent. Not all called for jury service sit; some seek exemptions, and jurisdictions vary about the ease with which one can avoid jury duty. Only in 1975 did the Supreme Court hold that, in criminal cases, women cannot be presumptively excluded from a pool of jurors. Taylor v. Louisiana, 419 U.S. 522 (1975).

Assuming one remains in the jury venire, the next question is whether one will be asked to participate in a given case. This process is called empaneling the jury. The choice of who will be empaneled is made by *voir dire* (to speak truth). Either judges or lawyers for the parties examine prospective jurors, who are asked a series of questions. Although the issue has been a subject of controversy, with periodic efforts made to alter the rule, judges in the federal courts typically conduct the voir dire. See Fed. R. Civ. P. 47; Fed. R. Crim. P. 24(a). The parties' counsel submit proposed questions in advance, and judges are required under certain limited circumstances to ask about areas of prejudice. Compare Ham v. South Carolina, 409 U.S. 524 (1973), with Rosales–Lopez v. United States, 451 U.S. 182 (1981). For example, capital defendants have a right to have inquiries made about racial prejudice. In general, in the federal system, the process is done very quickly. One study estimated that federal judges spent, on the average, from 30 to 60 minutes to empanel a jury. In contrast, in some state courts, lawyers conduct the voir dire, and the questioning is sometimes extensive.

While the theoretical purpose of the voir dire is to search for impartial jurors, in practice each side is looking for sympathetic decisionmakers. Litigants can make two kinds of challenges to jurors. One is a challenge "for cause"—that there is reason to believe that a given juror would not impartially decide an issue. A second is a "peremptory" challenge. Each side is permitted a specified number of challenges for which no reasons need be given. See Fed. R. Civ. P. 47; Fed. R. Crim. P. 24. One of the utilities of peremptory challenges is not having to explain (in front of other prospective or selected jurors or an opponent) the reasons for exclusion of a given individual. (For example, one might be concerned about an individual's mental capacities.) But the concern about preemptory challenges is that they will be used to exclude some jurors based on impermissible reasons, such as their race or sex. See Batson v. Kentucky, 476 U.S. 79 (1986); J.E.B. v. Alabama ex rel. T.B., 511 U.S. 127 (1994).

Note further that challenges to jurors' impartiality are best made at the time of selection. Post-conviction attacks must survive several rules of deference, some stemming from judicial interpretation and others from congressional directives. See Coleman v. Thompson, 501 U.S. 722 (1991); the Antiterrorism and Effective Death Penalty Act of 1996 (AEDPA).

Litigants with resources sometimes attempt to use sophisticated methods to learn about the attitudes of prospective jurors. One issue that has sparked a great deal of litigation is the question of what attitude prospective jurors have towards the imposition of the death penalty. In 1968, in Witherspoon v. Illinois, 391 U.S. 510 (1968), the Court held that the Sixth and Fourteenth Amendments were violated when all prospective jurors were dismissed for cause if they expressed objections to capital punishment. However, in 1985 the Court cut back on the *Witherspoon* rule. See Wainwright v. Witt, 469 U.S. 412 (1985).

This discussion highlights only some of the many issues that swirl around decisionmaking by juries. Other concerns deserve mention—including the questions of how much and what kinds of information jurors should receive. Recent Supreme Court decisions have enhanced judges' power to serve as gatekeepers by authorizing judges to screen expert testimony before it can be presented to a jury. Opponents of this ruling (known by the case's name, *Daubert*) argue that judges have a poor track record in understanding the nuances of science and that a restrictive approach has served to undermine access to courts and rights to jury trials. Another debate focuses on the degree of discretion that jurors should have when awarding damages, both compensatory and punitive. Yet other topics include whether jurors should be accessible to the press for interviews, whether jurors should be permitted to take notes and ask questions, and whether jurors ought to have and to use the power to "nullify" the law by acquitting defendants.

But two aspects of jury decisionmaking are not disputed. First, the institution has a remarkably high saliency, both in the United States and abroad. Second, those who serve on juries report that their experiences engender positive feelings about the justice system. As a consequence, the jury is understand as an important facet of the American political system, with its remarkable insistence that, in this democracy, individuals who are not government officials ought, upon occasion, to hold the state's power of judgment.

C. Controlling Judges

How do people become judges? In the United States, a quick but correct response is that politics is the primary route for becoming a judge. Electoral politics play a key role, whether in federal or state judicial selection. Defenders of this system argue that it provides for democratic input upfront and for a system that is more transparent and potentially more fair than highly centralized selection mechanisms. Critics argue that politics plays too great a role, making judicial positions less attractive and less legitimate.

On the federal side, life-tenured judges are nominated by the President and confirmed by the Senate. The respective arenas of authority between the President and the Senate are much disputed, as high profile nomination battles make plain the stakes of this unique job. But remember that these days, at the trial level in the federal system, the statutory judges (bankruptcy and magistrate judges) gain their positions through selection by life-tenured judges. Each of the federal circuit courts appoints bankruptcy judges for renewable 14-year terms, while district courts, with advice from selection panels, appoint magistrate judges for renewable 8-year terms. Further, the more than 2,000 judges who serve as Administrative Law Judges obtain their jobs via a competitive exam as well as a point system, which as noted, accords preferences to veterans.

On the state side, many judges are elected, although often for long terms and sometimes through retention elections. Contemporary concerns focus on the financing of elections, the increased use of advertising, and the degree to which national groups (identified as either pro-plaintiff or pro-defendant) attempt to effect outcomes in different states. The Supreme Court recently struck (5–4) a state provision from Minnesota that had limited what candidates for judicial office could say, but questions remain about whether a narrower regulation might survive First Amendment challenges. See Republican Party of Minnesota v. White, 536 U.S. 765 (2002).

How are judges controlled? A central mechanism to limit judicial power is the right to appeal, discussed in Chapter I. In addition to review of the decisions rendered, other mechanisms exist to constrain judges.

A first is that, just as a juror may not be appropriate to sit on a particular case, so may a judge be the wrong person to render judgment in a specific case. When judges *recuse* themselves, they need not give any reason. Alternatively, litigants can challenge a judge's impartiality. In the federal system, litigants can either move for disqualification based on particular evidence or based on several specified statutory grounds, such as that the judge has a financial stake (as in owning stock) affected by a lawsuit, or has a certain familial relationship to parties, or other grounds raising questions about the appearance or fact of impartiality. See 28 U.S.C. §§ 144, 455. The motions are made to the very judge challenged, although some districts have the practice of referring such questions to other judges.

At the lower echelons of the federal courts, decisions about recusal may be reviewed by hierarchically superior judges, although denials of motions for recusal are generally not appealable interlocutorily. Unhappy litigants must either await the conclusion of a lawsuit, obtain certification from the trial court and permission from the appellate court to appeal, or attempt mandamus. At the Supreme Court level, individual justices make the decisions, and no other body reviews those judgments.

In addition to motions for recusal, some states provide for peremptory challenges of judges. Each litigant may be permitted to request that a judge remove herself or himself from presiding in a case. Typically, a single peremptory challenge per side is permitted. See, e.g., Cal. Civ. Proc. Code § 170.6.

Jurisdictions often have disciplinary mechanisms that are external to the structure of a particular lawsuit. Article III of the United States Constitution provides one example. Federal judges have life tenure only "during good Behavior." Article II, § 4 provides that "all civil Officers of the United States, shall be removed from Office on Impeachment for, and Conviction of, Treason, Bribery, or other high Crimes and Misdemeanors." Given the enormity of the sanction, impeachments of federal judges are rare.

Because of the relative infrequency of impeachment and the ongoing concern about judicial misconduct, many have suggested that alternatives be developed. In 1980, Congress responded by enacting the Judicial Conduct and Disability Act, 28 U.S.C. § 372, which provides a mechanism for complainants to bring claims against sitting federal judges. Investigation and deliberation powers are given to the judiciary, which acts in private. If misconduct is found, the Judicial Council of the circuit in which the judge sits may take action or may refer the complaint and the record to the Judicial Conference of the United States. As remedies, the Act permits the Judicial Council or Judicial Conference to urge that a judge retire, to decline to assign cases to her or to him, or to censure a judge in public or in private. The desirability of such disciplinary mechanisms depends, in some measure, upon one's view of the frequency of misbehavior and of the ability to correct misbehavior without chilling judicial independence. Many states also have accountability mechanisms, such as discipline review boards and evaluations of judges through surveys of lawyers or litigants.

Another possible constraint is a civil lawsuit against a judge. While the Supreme Court has held that injunctive relief is available against judges (see Pulliam v. Allen, 466 U.S. 522 (1984)), the Court has prohibited awards of monetary damages against judges who act within their judicial capacity unless one can show a "clear absence of all jurisdiction." Stump v. Sparkman, 435 U.S. 349, 357 (1978). *Stump* provides a vivid example of the judicial immunity rule. A young woman claimed that a judge had ordered her sterilized and that no formal procedures in the state provided for the judge to do so. Nonetheless, the Supreme Court held the judge immune. The justifications for such immunity are the societal need for judges to act free from concern about personal consequences, the potentially large number of complainants who might seek to sue, and the availability of alternative remedies such as appellate review.

In addition to formal mechanisms, less formal constraints operate as well. In August 1972, the House of Delegates of the American Bar Association promulgated a Code of Judicial Conduct. Judicial canons may provide grounds for charging judges in misconduct proceedings, but the more important use is to provide statements of what constitutes appropriate behavior. Some states have adopted ethical codes for judges, as has the Judicial Conference of the United States Courts. Judges may also seek advice from committees of their colleagues on whether a proposed action falls within ethical boundaries. Moreover, while not articulated in writing, informal morés do much to shape those who hold the judicial office. Federal and state judges regularly meet in a variety of settings and are socialized by their peers, as well as by the commentary from the public and specialists who report, respond to, and criticize judicial actions.

Expectations of judges are not constant. Decades ago, many jurisdictions found it inappropriate for judges to encourage litigants to settle cases. The view was that judges ought not be directly involved in such efforts. Today, in many jurisdictions, procedural rules oblige judges to propose that litigants explore settlement. Other issues that have prompted debate and different answers across jurisdictions and time include whether judges must make public reporting of their finances, whether judges ought not to belong to clubs that exclude certain individuals based on race or sex, and whether judges ought to accept payments for travel and lodging to attend educational programs, sometimes provided by foundations associated with particular social or political issues.

Judicial behavior may be shaped by other factors. Some judges may impose their own restraints on what they write or how they judge because they are interested in gaining promotion, from trial court to appellate court and from appellate court to the Supreme Court. Even life tenure does not insulate judges from pursuing their own forms of career advancement. Outsiders may also seek to influence judicial behavior, through targeted attacks on judges based on their rulings. A few high-profile occurrences—involving efforts by organized groups to unseat specific judges because of their decisions on death penalty cases, habeas corpus petitions, or other questions—have prompted a series of conferences and special commissions to examine how to maintain an independent judiciary and how to enable public support for the concept of judicial freedom to render decisions that may prove to be controversial or unpopular. This problem is a concern for all systems, even when judges have life-tenure. But the problem becomes more acute when judges are subject to re-election or re-appointment.

D. The Centrality of Lawyers, the Costs of Process, and the Availability of Subsidies

Procedural systems depend on expertise. Even when a process is relatively informal, those who have experience with its parameters can gain advantage from that familiarity. The "repeat player" phenomenon, a term coined decades ago by Professor Marc Galanter, also permits repeat players to "play for the rules" by participating in structuring a process to maximize their advantage.

Some litigants—such as governments and large commercial actors—are repeat players, as are lawyers, who populate and profit from procedural systems. Hence, understanding the roles played by lawyers and how lawyers are paid is required for thinking about the structure and desirability of forms of process. Below, I sketch the federal constitutional parameters of the right to counsel in criminal and civil litigation, the relevant statutory provisions, and then turn to the private contractual relationships between lawyers and clients and to methods of court-based fee shifting, either from defendant to plaintiff or among a group of plaintiffs.

On the criminal side, the lack of equilibrium between government and individual defendants generated concern about the integrity of criminal judgments. The United States Constitution was reread to require equipage—counsel (in Gideon v. Wainwright, 372 U.S. 335 (1963)), investigative and expert capacity (Ake v. Oklahoma, 470 U.S. 68 (1985)), disclosure (in Brady v. Maryland, 373 U.S. 83 (1963)), and subsidies for appeal when offered by states (in Douglas v. California, 372 U.S. 353 (1963))—all in response to a shared sense of the illegitimacy of outcomes borne from deeply unequal resources.

Many of these constitutional rights are implemented by statutes. In the federal system, for example, Congress has, through the Criminal Justice Act (CJA), required that each federal district court have a "plan for furnishing representation for any person financially unable to obtain adequate representation." 18 U.S.C. § 3006A(a). Specifically, subsection (b) provides for counsel either by "a panel of attorneys designated or approved by the court, or from a bar association, legal aid agency, or defender organization furnishing representation pursuant to the plan", upon a sharing of financial inability to obtain counsel. Payment rates are low— under $75—as compared to the private market. In addition, the CJA provides for government-funded "investigation, expert, or other services necessary for adequate representation," again with presumptive caps. 18 U.S.C. § 3006A(c).

The civil justice system has been more reluctant to adopt a parallel attitude towards litigants within it. Characterized as focusing on "private" interactions among disputants, the civil justice system assumes a certain fungibility of litigants that is foreign to the criminal justice system, in which the state is always the prosecutor. If the rules of civil procedure sometimes tilt towards plaintiffs (for example, when evaluating complaints for dismissal) or towards defendants (for example, when imposing burdens of proof), neutrality results from the assumption that plaintiffs and defendants are themselves revolving sets of players, sometimes plaintiffs and other times defendants, changing from one case to another. The brunt of whatever assistance any rule affords to one of a civil suit will over time be felt by all, thereby providing reassurance about legitimacy.

But even the civil justice system has its moments when pricing access to its processes makes the inequality of resources between litigants too much to bear. The veil of ignorance that assumes any person could be either plaintiff or defendant is pierced (if not lifted). Subsidies and wealth transfers within litigation—such as the waiver of filing fees, the provision of lawyers, the payment for development of expert information, or shifting costs among litigants—are provided. The means vary—from public funding, to taxing lawyers by requiring contributions from attorney trust accounts, to requiring that costs be reallocated within a specific litigation. These principles emanate from constitutional interpretation, statutory law, and procedural rulemaking.

A first example comes from the 1971 decision of Boddie v. Connecticut, 401 U.S. 371. The Supreme Court held that at least in the case of divorce, the state had (as a matter of equal protection, due process, or some ill-defined mixture of the two) to subsidize a litigant too poor to pay state-imposed filing fees. For some, *Boddie's* rule suggested that pricing entry to courts (even in terms of imposing below-cost filing fees) was similarly unfair and unconstitutional in other contexts.

But the Court thereafter reasserted that the system takes litigants as it finds them, and if litigants cannot make their own way into the system, that problem is not one that the Constitution solves. Hence, the Court refused to require a waiver of filing fees when welfare recipients sought judicial review of a reduction in benefits, and the Court refused state-subsidized access to a proposed bankruptcy petitioner alleging inability to pay the filing fee. See, e.g. United States v. Kras, 409 U.S. 434 (1973).

Subsidizing filing fees for divorces is not the only example of constitutional alteration of the unaided access premise. The relatively few other instances stem from cases in which the state litigates against individuals and the issues at stake are—in substantive due process terms—"fundamental." Thus, in quasi-criminal proceedings (such as civil commitment processes in which loss of physical liberty is possible), counsel may be provided for an impoverished litigant from public funds. Similarly, prisoners cannot be deprived of all access to courts, although the means required to be made available has recently been narrowed.

One other litigation posture—cases in which the state attempts to create or to terminate parental rights—has also been recognized by federal courts as requiring, as a matter of constitutional law, litigation subsidies. In Lassiter v. Department of Social Services, 452 U.S. 18 (1981), the Supreme Court concluded that, by virtue of the Due Process Clause, persons facing loss of the legal status of being a parent have the right, under limited circumstances, to be given state-subsidized counsel. Embedded within that conclusion was a more general assertion (actually, a rejection of a view) that impoverished civil litigants in general do not have a constitutional right to counsel.

Subsidies for disputes about parental status are provided not only at times to fund lawyers but also to fund the production of certain forms of evidence and to assist when litigants seek appellate review. In Little v. Streater, 452 U.S. 1 (1981), the Court required state-subsidized genetic testing when states sought to impose paternity obligations on putative fathers. And, more recently, in the 1996 ruling of M.L.B. v. S.L.J., 519 U.S. 102 (1996), the Court required states to provide transcripts to enable appellate review of termination of parental rights. To require a subsidy for this kind of litigant, and then only for this kind of litigant, prompted the Court to thread a complex path in light of contemporary equal protection and due process law. The Court concluded that its ruling (mandating funds for transcripts to enable appeals in termination cases) did not make "state aid to subsidize privately initiated action" generally available nor did it require the alleviation of the "consequences of differences in economic circumstances that existed apart from state action." Id. at 120–121.

To summarize, save for such occasional exceptions, judges have not read the Constitution of the United States to require substantial inroads into the premise of unaided access to court for civil litigants. Which is not, of course, to say that no aid to civil litigants is provided but rather that little aid is provided through constitutional interpretation. State courts have many times read their own constitutions more broadly. But equipage for civil litigants—from filing fees to investigation to counsel to experts—is generally left either to the legislature or to the market. The Legal Services Corporation (LSC) (with its restrictive regulations), statutory fee-shifting, and in forma pauperis statutes (with circumscribed rights for prisoners and increasingly demanding evidentiary requirements) provide the current federal legislative responses to the problems of poor people seeking to interact with the civil justice litigation system. Contingent fees and privately-funded organizations must do the rest.

Specifically, the Legal Services Corporation Act of 1974, 42 U.S.C. §§ 2996 et seq., created the Legal Services Corporation as a non-profit government-funded corporation, "for the purpose of providing financial support for legal assistance in noncriminal proceedings or matters to persons financially unable to afford legal assistance." 42 U.S.C. § 2996b(a). LSC makes grants to hundreds of local organizations that provide free legal assistance to between 1,000,000 and 2,000,000 indigent clients annually. Many grantees are funded by a combination of public and private sources, and they are governed by local Boards of Directors that establish policies and priorities.

LSC funds come with restrictions. For example, LSC funds cannot be used for most criminal proceedings, political activities, and litigation involving nontherapeutic abortion, desegregation, or military desertion. See 42 U.S.C. §§ 2996f(b)(1)–(10). Additional limitations were added in 1996. Programs that receive federal funds cannot generally lobby for legal changes, bring class actions, or represent incarcerated clients.

The imposition of such restrictions prompted internal controversies for grantees of the LSC: Should they abide by them? Challenge them? Turn to private funding? Would challenges prompt further cutbacks? One group of lawyers employed by grantees of the Legal Services Corporation, joined by indigent clients and contributors to LSC programs, filed suit, arguing that the First Amendment precluded Congress from imposing such restrictions on the attorney-client relationship and from intruding on lawyers' autonomy and ability to exercise professional judgment when working with clients. In 2001, the United States Supreme Court agreed in part that one of the funding conditions, prohibiting LSC-funded lawyers from attempts "to amend or otherwise challenge existing welfare law," violated the First Amendment. See Legal Services Corp. v. Velazquez, 531 U.S. 533, 533 (2001). The Justices in the majority (Stevens, Kennedy, Souter, Ginsburg, and Breyer) held that the restriction effectively prohibited "advice or argumentation that existing welfare laws are unconstitutional or unlawful." 531 U.S. at 547.

Turn then to the private market. Some commentators believe that, because lawyers have a state-created monopoly to provide certain services, they should be required to provide some of those services for free, *pro bono.* Others have identified the potential to use lawyers' professional dues to subsidize services for the poor. And some states require lawyers, obliged to segregate clients' funds in interest-bearing accounts, to pool the interest that is too small to make reimbursement to clients economically feasible and to use it for legal services for the poor. These Interest Earned on Lawyer Trust Accounts (IOLTA) have generated hundreds of millions of dollars for legal services and have also become the focal point of litigation. Attorneys opposed to such uses challenged state statutes as illegal "takings." In 1998, the Supreme Court agreed that the small sums were "property" requiring additional analysis as to what form of compensation was "just." Phillips v. Washington Legal Foundation, 524 U.S. 156 (1998). Thereafter, 5–4, the Supreme Court upheld the constitutionality of IOLTA programs based on the view that the taking was justified by the public use provided through paying for legal services and that no compensation was required as clients suffered no net losses. See Brown v. Legal Foundation of Washington, 123 S.Ct. 1406 (2003).

Yet other options include insurance for legal fees, either as a free-standing product or tied to the purchase of insurance for one's car or home. Most policies for car insurance, for example, include provisions that, if accidents occur, the insurance carrier will represent the insured but will also control the decisions on litigation and settlement. Some associations and unions offer forms of legal services, as do some legal "clinics," providing certain kinds of services at reduced rates.

Economists model how the various systems operate in an effort to ascertain what rules are optimal for aligning the incentives of lawyers and clients and for achieving private enforcement of rights without inspiring too many claims of questionable validity. How such rules work in practice depends on many variables, including whether litigants and their lawyers are "risk averse" or "risk prone," the procedural opportunities available to drive up or down costs, billing practices and customs, and the role of courts in superintending the strategic interaction of adversaries.

Finally, consider the purchase and sale of legal services through contracts entered into between lawyers and clients. Payment options include a lump sum for a particular kind of work, hourly rates, or contingent fees in which an attorney fronts the costs (to be repaid on conclusion) and gains a fee by taking a percentage of the plaintiff's recovery if successful. Given relatively little funding for legal services and exacting eligibility requirements, the contingent fee system enables lawyers to serve as lenders for clients otherwise unable to pursue litigation.

At the end of litigation, in some countries, losers pay the winners' lawyers fees, often limited by a schedule of approved amounts. In the federal courts here, with the entry of judgment, a court usually requires the loser to pay the winner's *costs*, defined under 28 U.S.C. § 1920 to include filing and witness fees, transcript costs and the like, but typically not attorneys' fees. Fed. R. Civ. P. 54. In terms of fees, the United States tradition (sometimes called "the American Rule") has been for each side to pay its own attorneys' fees, but that practice has several exceptions, some statutory and some stemming from courts' equitable or inherent powers. Hundreds of statutes authorize judges to require losing parties to pay the lawyers' fees of prevailing parties. The Civil Rights Attorney's Fee Act of 1976, 42 U.S.C. § 1988, is one example, which involves one-way fee shifts. Losing defendants have to pay winning plaintiffs but losing plaintiffs only pay winning defendants if the case was filed in bad faith. Other fee-shifting statutes are two-way shifts, in which whoever loses pays the opponent's fees.

In addition to such statutory provisions, courts may use their equitable powers to require groups of plaintiffs to share fees if the lead plaintiff creates a "common fund" or confers a benefit on a group, such as in a class action. In recent years, a few judges have "auctioned" large-scale cases by requiring lawyers to provide bids, setting fees in advance. Courts also have authority to shift fees when a filing is made in bad faith.

Whether by statutory mandate or equitable powers, a distinct question is how to calculate the amount of fees due. Absent parties' agreement, courts often assess fees based on a *lodestar* (hours times rate) or on a percentage of the recovery. Disputes about fees sometimes result in additional litigation. As judges award and assess fees, they gain insight into the high costs of litigation and sometimes into attorney excesses.

To summarize, a central problem for all legal systems is how to equip participants and how to respond to the disparate resources of disputants. Be clear that equipage is a problem for all systems, whether court-based or not. I have focused here on court-based processes but the issues are also acute in administrative proceedings and in ADR. Contemporary debates in the United States about the enforcement of contracts mandating arbitration in lieu of litigation between employees and employers and between consumers and manufacturers address the question of who pays for the cost of these private dispute resolution systems. Green Tree Financial Corp. v. Randolph, 531 U.S. 79 (2000). Further, researchers in England have demonstrated that many individuals see law as relevant to their problems, but eight out of ten did not use either courts or administrative tribunals, or ombudspersons. While the venues for process have multiplied, many potential disputants have no access to that array.

VII. RULEMAKING

Procedural systems rely on rules. Mastery of procedure requires mastery of rules. Lawyers tend to have relevant rulebooks on their desks, but by the time students have graduated from law school, they have internalized much of the structure and content of procedural rules as a language.

Gaining fluency in that language was once simpler than it is today. For much of the twentieth century, the term "procedure" served as a reference to the processes by which courts made decisions. Courts were assumed to be institutions focused singularly on adjudication, and proceduralists were, in turn, focused exclusively on courts. Moreover, during the second half of the twentieth century, the Federal Rules of Civil Procedure, promulgated by the United States Supreme Court in 1938, provided the dominant model for rulemaking, as more than half the states adopted them and Congress deferred to judicial branch processes for their modification.

But by the end of the twentieth century, courts no longer provided only adjudication but also offered an array of other processes. Lawyers and judges had become increasingly critical of the 1938 rules; states had forged their own paths, and Congress had itself become a font of rulemaking through statutes focused on specific kinds of cases or litigants. Moreover, many venues (including administrative agencies in the public sector, arbitration and other dispute resolution programs in the private sector, and transnational bodies) had become central sources of procedural rulemaking and invention.

How are those interested in procedure to respond? I suggest a threefold response. One is to become familiar with a single set of integrated rules, to understand how they respond to problems common to all procedural systems. To that end, the Federal Rules of Civil Procedure have served here as an exemplary set, contrasted with federal criminal rules. But, and second, be clear that rules for all procedural systems have to address the same problems: What kind of information must be provided to opponents and to decisionmakers? What degree of autonomy is permitted to disputants in structuring disputes, gathering information, and making claims? How can strategic interaction be contained? What powers are given to and imposed on decisionmakers? Proceduralists are thus also comparativists, analyzing differing responses to shared problems.

Third, all proceduralists should grapple with the interrelationships and interdependencies of procedure and substance. Therefore, the question of how to allocate the power of rulemaking itself is a central problem for proceduralists. In the United States federal system, the questions include the propriety of locating rulemaking authority in the judiciary and of giving the Chief Justice and the Supreme Court prominent roles, the special role of lawyers in process design, the desirability of congressional intervention or generativity, the role for case-by-case adjustments by judges and for popular input by an array of constituencies, and the sources of innovation in procedure.

One must remember that the dominance of court-generated Federal Rules was concurrent with a focus on federal regulatory mechanisms to build the nation. The diminishing centrality of those rules comes not only from the problems of their being created before photocopies and computers were commonplace but also from shifts in political understandings of the desirability of private ordering. Thus, many agendas beyond rulemaking shape whatever rules are made.

A. Generating Rules Within the Federal System

Procedural rules can be governed by local or national law and can be created by either courts or legislatures. At first, in the United States, federal court rules mirrored those of states. During later eras, national uniformity—sometimes through statutes and at other times by court-based rulemaking—came to be the norm. Yet local variations have also persisted.

With the First Judiciary Act of 1789, the federal courts were required to conform their procedures to the states in which the federal court sat. Litigants in federal courts in Connecticut, for example, followed that state's practice, distinct from how one proceeded in the federal courts in

New York or in Vermont. During the nineteenth century, Congress authorized a dynamic, rather than a static, conformity—permitting federal courts to update their rules as state practices changed. In addition, distinct federal rules for equity began to develop, and Congress provided by statute some specific rules for certain kinds of proceedings.

During the twentieth century, as part of many efforts at nationalization, federal rules crossed the boundaries of states. In 1912, uniform Rules of Equity were promulgated, but the more profound shift came two decades later, when in 1934, Congress enacted the Rules Enabling Act (REA), authorizing the United States Supreme Court to make rules for all civil cases. That statute was hotly debated, with populists concerned about its ability to shift power away from states towards the federal system. The resultant Federal Rules of Civil Procedure did, indeed, become the template for the nation and the major procedural reform of the twentieth century.

Under the 1934 statute (now codified as modified at 28 U.S.C. §§ 2071–2077), the Supreme Court gained the power to promulgate rules of practice and procedure that, absent an affirmative legislative override, become effective nationwide. To create the first rules, the Court turned to experts—lawyers and judges. In 1935, the Supreme Court appointed an Advisory Committee to draft civil rules. William Mitchell, the chair, a former Attorney General of the United States, was a member of a law firm in Minnesota. Other members were from the bar and were active in the American Bar Association and the American Law Institute (ALI). The academics on the Committee included Charles Clark (reporter and then Dean of Yale Law School), Armistead Doble (Dean of the University of Virginia Law School), Edmund Morgan (of Harvard Law School and a reporter for the ALI's model Penal Code of Evidence), and Edson Sunderland (of Michigan Law School). The Committee drafted rules that, with some modifications, were accepted by the Supreme Court. In 1937, the Supreme Court promulgated the Federal Rules of Civil Procedure, which became effective in 1938.

The 1938 Rules of Civil Procedure (detailed in the linear description of a lawsuit provided in Chapter I) represented a commitment to nationalization, to uniformity, to expertise, and to simplification. To accomplish those goals, the rules collapsed prior procedures that had taken different shapes depending upon whether a claim sought legal or equitable relief. A single set of rules—transsubstantive in their reach— governed regardless of the kind of relief requested or the basis for the cause of action.

The new rules relaxed pleading requirements but imposed obligations on adversaries to exchange information— both written and oral—about the facts and law in dispute. The concept of lawyers and judges meeting (the pre-trial) was borrowed from practices of state courts and the English system, whereas the mandated disclosure of information (discovery, accomplished through interrogatories, in-person depositions, production of documents, examination of physical evidence, and admissions) was largely an invention of the 1938 Rules. Under the Rules, trial judges gained substantial discretion to tailor processes to the circumstances of a particular case. To do so, judges and lawyers were permitted to discuss cases in advance of the formal moments of arguing disputed motions or going to trial.

The scholarly and legal currents that supported this project have been conceptualized (at least in hindsight) as a progressive reform project promoted by individuals having faith in facts, expertise, and government. The reworkings of procedural systems and the focus on federal adjudication were concurrent with a larger movement committed to governance through increasing reliance on federal courts to enforce national norms in a milieu appreciative of managerial expertise. Constitutional interpretation looked favorably upon court-based processes; statutory provisions were understood as preferring adjudication to other forms of disposition, and courts were committed to streamlining and "modernizing" their processes to meet growing demands.

The federal procedural rulemakers were evangelistic about their work product, and they proudly argued for its emulation. For several decades, they succeeded, as their model of procedure was admired and its aegis expanded. More than half of the states revised their rules of court to resemble those within the federal system. The 1938 rule packet remained largely intact for some forty years. And, when the first significant changes were made in the 1960s, their purpose was to expand on the 1938 premises. Rule drafters revised multi-party practice, and especially the class action rule, to facilitate aggregation of parties and claims. Courts also adopted individual calendar systems so that a judge assigned at the outset of a case would have responsibility for it from filing to disposition, thereby enhancing judicial authority over its processing.

Further, during the 1960s and 1970s, the model provided by the Federal Rules was applied to the administrative context. The Supreme Court—borrowing Professor Charles Reich's insight that statutory entitlements were forms of "property" to be protected from state deprivation by "due process of law"—required that final decisionmaking about individual entitlements employ judicial modes of process to ensure fairness. This adjudicatory model relied on a belief in the utility of the adversary system and on a commitment to making its processes more readily available to a range of users.

But the method for drafting the rules, even during the heady days celebrating their ingenuity, was not static. In the 1950s, under the leadership of Chief Justice Warren, the process by which the rules came into being was changed. The Advisory Committee on rules was placed under the Judicial Conference of the United States, the body of under thirty judges, including the chief judge of each circuit and a district judge elected for a term from each circuit, with the Chief Justice presiding. 28 U.S.C. § 331. As initially conceived, the revision of the Rules Enabling Act would have given the Judicial Conference the power to transmit the rules to Congress, thereby bypassing the Supreme Court and avoiding many of the problems (constitutional and otherwise) of using the Court in the rulemaking process. But the Chief Justice thought it necessary to keep the Supreme Court involved.

As a result, and as modified in the 1980s, the advisory committees draft the rules and transmit them to a standing committee which, if concurring, then sends them on to the Judicial Conference. If the Judicial Conference approves proposed changes, it transmits them to the Supreme Court. The Supreme Court reviews the rule changes and, if in accord, transmits them to Congress no later than May 1 of a given year. 28 U.S.C. § 2074(a). The rules then become effective unless Congress takes some contrary action by December 1 of that year. See 28 U.S.C. § 2074(a).

Questions about the scope and range of rules have been ever present. The Rules Enabling Act, 28 U.S.C. § 2072, gives the Court "the power to prescribe general rules of practice and procedure ... and evidence" for the district courts. 28 U.S.C. § 2072(b) states a principle—that the rulemaking power cannot be used to "abridge, enlarge, or modify any substantive right." The second part of § 2072(b) is known as the supercession clause and was enacted in 1934 to help the new rules sweep away inconsistent provisions nested in the myriad of federal statutes. A parallel provision, 18 U.S.C. § 3771, gives the Court rulemaking power for criminal rules, and a first national set was promulgated in 1946.

The issues include whether the Court has the expertise to make rules for lower courts, whether the rules are a form of legislation, and whether a distinction between procedure and substance is workable. Because, the Supreme Court's role is pivotal but ill-defined, members of the Court have varied in their reaction to this obligation. Some justices consider the wisdom of particular proposals and either approve, reject, or write brief comments to accompany transmittal of the rules. Others see the task as ministerial—conveying the work of the Judicial Conference to Congress. Yet other Justices have objected to the Court's involvement and have questioned the constitutionality and the wisdom of rules coming from the Court and then returning to the Court if their legality is questioned.

During the Watergate crisis, with evidence of government efforts at the highest levels to cover up wrongdoings, the rulemaking process came under more public scrutiny. As Watergate was unfolding in the early 1970s, the Court presented Congress with the first-ever set of Federal Rules of Evidence. Included were provisions for evidentiary privileges that would have shielded certain government officials from being required to testify. Relying on its powers under the Rules Enabling Act, Congress delayed the entire project for some three years. In the wake of those events, concerns returned about both the substantive agendas that rules could forward and about the role of the Chief Justice. When the Evidence Rules were finally effective in 1975, they contained no federal privileges but instead deferred to state law on that question.

B.   Restructuring the Process and Reallocating Authority

Criticism about the processes for rulemaking intersected with critiques of the rules themselves, as a larger debate emerged about the use of litigation to generate and to enforce legal norms. By the 1970s and 1980s, the import of the 1966 revisions of the class action rule (enabling self-appointed individuals and their lawyers as representatives to bring cases on behalf of hundreds or thousands of others, similarly situated, who might not know or be able individually to pursue claims of right) and of discovery rules (permitting access to documents that revealed evidence of the harms caused by lead paint, asbestos, and other products) had heightened awareness of the effects of procedure on substantive rights.

As a consequence, during the last two decades of the twentieth century, the premises of the 1938 Rules were dismantled in several respects. The assumption that rule-making was the province of expert technocrats faded, as did the progressive faith in expertise itself. In 1988, Congress amended the REA to require that rules (for courts other than the Supreme Court) be prescribed "only after giving appropriate public notice and an opportunity for comment." 28 U.S.C. § 2071(b). Committee meetings must now be open, and recommendations for changes must be accompanied by written reports including dissenters' views. 28 U.S.C. § 2073(c). Further, Congress enlarged the time for popular input after the Court transmits rules from ninety days to six months. 28 U.S.C. § 2074. And, as is detailed below, Congress took up rulemaking itself, thereby undercutting a system of transsubstantive rules.

In 1990, Congress returned to civil justice through enactment of the Civil Justice Reform Act, 28 U.S.C. §§ 471–482 (known as the CJRA or the Biden Bill, after its proponent, Senator Joseph Biden). That legislation, which expired in 1997, required local district courts to convene advisory groups to review dockets and devise district-specific plans for "expense and delay reduction." Congress asked the advisory groups to consider developing different procedures for cases of different complexity, mandating extensive judicial management of pretrial activity including discovery, authorizing referrals to alternative dispute resolution programs, and encouraging settlements. Some of the plans were incorporated as appendices to the local rules of districts, becoming a source of inter-district disuniformity.

One commentator argued that Article III required courts to retain control over rulemaking and thus that the CJRA was unconstitutional. That minority view has not persuaded others, who rely on a mixture of history and case law for the proposition that shared, rather than exclusive, powers are both constitutional and desirable. Indeed, a leading case on congressional power to delegate authority—Mistretta v. United States, 488 U.S. 361 (1989)—upheld the creation of the United States Sentencing Commission, which includes judges and nonjudges and which promulgates guidelines constraining judicial discretion to such a degree (some argue) that they have the power of legislation. In passing, the *Mistretta* opinion noted the analogy of the guideline system to federal rulemaking.

In some legislation, Congress continued to endorse judicial rulemaking. For example, in the early 1990s, Congress delegated to the federal courts some power over appellate jurisdiction. Federal rules are not themselves supposed to alter the jurisdiction of the courts, which is established by the Constitution and by Congress. However, Congress instructed courts to determine when an order of a district court is "final" for the purposes of appellate jurisdiction by amending 28 U.S.C. § 2072(c) so that courts' rulemaking authority includes "defining when a ruling of a district court is final for the purposes of appeal under § 1291," and by amending Section 1292(e) to permit the Supreme Court to "prescribe rules in accordance with § 2072 ... to provide for an appeal of an interlocutory decision to the courts of appeals that is not otherwise provided for" under Section 1292.

On the other hand, during the 1990s, Congress also took an increasingly active role in making rules itself. For example, in the Civil Rights Act of 1991, Congress sought to facilitate intervention (governed by Fed. R. Civ. P. 24) in employment discrimination cases. In the 1995 Private Securities Reform Act, Congress changed class action processes for securities cases. The Prison Litigation Reform Act of 1996 altered the provisions for appointing special masters (pursuant to Fed. R. Civ. P. 53) in prison conditions cases.

Moreover, in the Antiterrorism and Effective Death Penalty Act of 1996 (AEDPA), Congress amended Rule 22 of the Federal Rules of Appellate Procedure, although not with any clarity. Rule 22 provides that, for appeals in habeas corpus cases, an appellant needs a "certificate of appealability" from either a district or appellate judge. Section 103 retains the provision that permits either a district or appellate judge to issue a "certificate of appealability" in a habeas proceeding. However, Section 102 amends 28 U.S.C. § 2253 (again dealing with appealability in habeas proceedings) to permit only appellate judges to issue certificates of appealability. According to the Administrative Office of the United States Courts, the discrepancies in drafting were brought to the attention of members of Congress, but to no avail. Congress also stated a standard of appealability; a proposed appellant had to make a "substantial showing of the denial of a constitutional right." AEDPA also created a special provision for making closed circuit television available to crime victims when criminal trials are moved out of state more than 350 miles from the place of the events. Congress was there responding to (and changing) a decision of the federal district judge presiding at the trial of Timothy McVeigh, convicted of bombing the Alfred P. Murrah federal building in Oklahoma City.

In 1996 Congress also amended the Civil Rights of Institutionalized Persons Act to limit prisoner litigation by altering the requirements for filing complaints. For prisoners to initiate suit directly, the Act mandates first exhausting all available administrative remedies. For the Attorney General (AG) to proceed, he or she must personally sign the complaint. The Act also alters criteria for intervention; if the AG wants to intervene in a pending case, the AG must certify a series of factual and legal allegations including why intervention by the United States is of general public importance. 42

U.S.C. § 1997c(b)(1). Congress further specified that, in addition to the criteria under Federal Rules Civil Procedure 12 for dismissal, courts can dismiss prisoner actions on their own motion upon finding a claim to be frivolous or malicious. 42 U.S.C. § 1997e(c). The Act required that, "to the extent practicable, . . . pretrial proceeding[s] in which the prisoner's participation is required or permitted shall be conducted by telephone, video conference, or other telecommunications technology without removing the prisoner from the facility in which the prisoner is confined." See 42 U. S. C § 1997e(f)(1).

Congress and the judiciary have also had new debates about the Federal Rules of Evidence. In 1994, the Supreme Court declined to promulgate a rule proposed by the Advisory Committee on the Rules of Evidence that would have altered Rule 412 to extend a "rape shield" rule (limiting the admissibility of evidence related to the prior sexual conduct of a victim) to civil cases. In that year, Congress enacted evidentiary Rules 413, 414, and 415, which provide for admissibility of certain kinds of evidence against defendants accused of sexual assault and child molestation and thereby alter the standards weighing the probative as compared to the prejudicial nature of evidence. See Pub. L. 103–332, 108 Stat. 2136 (Sept. 13, 1994).

In short, in a variety of contexts, Congress has crafted procedural rules linked to particular subject matter, thereby limiting the transsubstantivity of rules and judicial control over rulemaking. Further, the federal judiciary has also revisited transsubstantivity and has developed different procedures for habeas litigation and for "complex" litigation. Thus, lawyers who practice in the federal courts need to be sure that they know not only all of the relevant federal procedural and evidentiary rules as well as the local rules, but also whether specific statutes modify or alter the rules for a certain type of litigation.

C. The Diminishing Centrality of the Federal Rules

Thus far, I have focused on the Federal Rules and the growing criticism of both the processes for rulemaking and the content of the rules. But the critique is broader than the rules themselves. While some of the criticism is about the project's failure to make good on its own promises, others reject its animating premises. From a number of quarters and with a wide array of motives and goals comes a range of voices evidencing failing faith in adjudicatory procedure.

Some of the objections come from those committed to the rubric of adjudicatory civil processes but seeking to alter its format to take better account of problems of fairness—stemming from economic disparities, discrimination against individuals based on their identity, and the many challenges entailed in rendering legitimate judgments. One such objection faults the procedural system for not doing enough to facilitate rights-claiming. Given the centrality of lawyers and other repeat players to adversarial processing, large segments of the middle class—let alone the poor—are precluded from turning to process because of its costs. A related set of concerns, again voiced by those committed to the project of adjudication and wanting more of it, worries that courts are populated by governing elites inhospitable to claimants identified as occupying disfavored statuses. Although the demography of court users (both voluntary and involuntary) has shifted, the composition of judiciaries and of the legal profession has not changed as much.

Yet another source of concern about adjudication came from social science empiricism on decisionmaking and cognitive processes. As psychologists explore how individuals and groups make decisions, they interrogated procedural forms to assess whether to alter modes of presentation, rules of evidence, framing of information, and the numbers and background knowledge of decisionmakers.

Another critique moves somewhat away from the adjudicatory mode but does not debate its aspirations for easing access through simplification. Rather, under an umbrella of humanism, communitarianism, and social welfare concerns, a range of commentators have objected to the depersonalization, objectification, and distance that they associate with the formality of court processes and its dependency on legal professionals. Arguing for more user-friendly, less adversarial processes, posited as capable of producing more useful remediation, these critics want to re-center process on the disputants' voices and goals.

Alternative Dispute Resolution is the current movement embodying such concerns and stressing reliance on processes such as mediation and arbitration, argued to be more generative than adjudication. Illustrative is the name—"Just Resolutions"—chosen by the American Bar Association's ADR Section for its newsletter. While one aspect of this form of critique seeks to supplement and complement adjudication (captured by the metaphor of a multi-doored courthouse), another is hostile to trial processes. These critics view trials as requiring extravagant investments of resources to yield imperfect states of knowledge and unhappy participants.

A different kind of critique worries that the system has provided too much by way of opportunities for process. These concerns regard twentieth century aspirations for lawyer-based production of information to yield good and reliable outcomes as simplistic, superseded, or wrong. Critics point to how rules of discovery, crafted before photocopying and computers were commonplace, did not envision the massive amounts of information generated, stored, or hidden. Such rules have proven to be incentives for profits that lawyers garner from production and obfuscation and may well have played a role in restructuring the legal profession, now dominated by large law firms dependent on hourly billing. From this vantage point, class action and other aggregation rules were overly optimistic about the capacity to group similarly-situated individuals in collectives that could be adequately represented through a single or small number of self-elected or designated advocates. Strategic acting by attorneys for plaintiffs and by defendants in search of "global peace" yield judgments protecting both sets of interests at the expense of either those injured or the public.

Yet another set of objections is more technocratic, fastening on problems of sloppiness, inattention, ineptitude, inexperience, and misuse, all caused by lawyers with a range of motives and skills, engaged in strategic interaction. As the pre-trial process provided multiple opportunities for adversarial exchange, judges began to argue that oversight was needed and specifically that they should take on the role of manager. They saw in litigation problems of inefficiencies and analogized their problems to that of businesses, in need of being well-run through hierarchical structures.

In sum, the celebration of the 1938 Rules has been replaced with the language of crisis and the dissolution of some of the central tenets of those rules. The aspiration for transsubstantive uniformity of the 1938 Rules has been rejected—through amendments made by the judiciary, carving out special processes for different kinds of cases and detailing local and varying rule regimes; by Congress, requiring that certain litigants use subject-matter specific statutes; and by private contract, creating a multitude of dispute resolution programs. Further, transnational processes are of increasing relevance to the United States. The net result is that the Rules, once a centerpiece of a course called Civil Procedure, are no longer the only framework that those involved in civil disputing within the federal system need to understand.

Other pressures come from a different source: interest in expanding judicial modes by moving across borders. While procedure was once conceived as insular, and international procedures were assumed to be predicated on relationships among nations (public international law) or transnational corporate actors (private international law), those conceptual and legal barriers are lowering. Increasing interaction among professional classes, driven by both political and economic transactions, are diminishing the structural distinctions between civil and common law countries in professional training, career paths, and tasks for lawyers and judges.

Further, through increasing transnational trade and the nomenclature of "human rights," the framing of conflicts between individuals and states has moved beyond the boundaries of the nation-state. Political theorists in search of rights have conceptualized a small subset of claims as intrinsic to personhood. Based on theories of consent or of universal jurisdiction, they argue for their enforcement domestically or through international bodies. Moreover, from within the boundaries of some nation-states came groups of "First Nations," arguing that their sovereignty entailed control over their own dispute resolution processes as well as rights to proceed through national or international processes. International and regional treaties, some related to human rights and others focused on commercial transactions, deploy an array of dispute resolution mechanisms, ranging from adjudication (at the behest of either nation-states and, increasingly, individual complainants) to arbitration or settlement-focused processes.

Further, countries involved in trade and private corporate actors in transnational settings wanted reliable legal regimes. Thus, initiatives are underway to create procedural rules for civil disputes that cross jurisdictional lines. A series of covenants, promulgated through the United Nations, announce rights to fair and public hearings, aimed at protecting economic and personal security and at ensuring equality before the law. Reliance is placed on impartial and independent judges as the iconic protectors of the rule of law, working through transparent processes to which the public has access. For example, in 1985, in an effort to protect judges against the very governments that deploy them, the United Nations issued twenty "basic principles on the independence of the judiciary." Hoping for "effective implementation," the UN appointed a special rapporteur to monitor compliance through yearly reports addressing corruption, accountability, and independence.

The private sector is also playing an important role, as private organizations forge links among jurists and lawyers worldwide. Significant foundation support (from the Open Society Institute, the Ford Foundation, the World Bank, and others) has promoted judicial independence projects in efforts to use legal processes to enable societal and political development. Courts have also lent their voices through rulings—predicated upon a mixture of constitutional and natural law—that a judiciary has a right to independence. Some decisions have required budgets for courts to be insulated from politics or that terms of service for judges be fixed to limit executive and parliamentary control.

In addition to developing a shared jurisprudence of "the judicial," the UN, regional organizations, the World Bank, and other entities have created new dispute resolution mechanisms for specific problems (some stemming from treaties on trade, others focused on equality rights) that rely either on court-based or arbitral models. And, in the late 1990s, the American Law Institute (ALI), working in conjunction with the International Institute for the Unification of Private Law (UNIDROIT), launched an effort to draft principles and rules of "transnational civil procedure," adoptable by a country for adjudication of disputes arising from commercial transactions.

Building on earlier attempts by European procedural scholars (many involved with an international association of procedural law) to harmonize different legal regimes, ALI/UNIDROIT seeks to negotiate differing legal traditions (most prominently those of civil and common law procedures). The proposed regime bears some resemblance to model rules for arbitration but aspires to be court-based— standing in contrast to the proliferation of mini-procedural codes detailed through individual contracts in which parties opt out of government-based dispute resolution either by turning to arbitration organizations or by crafting their own dispute resolution mechanisms.

Thus, in contrast to traditional comparativist conceptions of "transplantation" of a distinct feature from one system to another, the newer efforts can be understood as forms of domestication and homogenization. Moreover, inside each country's own processes, influences of lawyers and litigants coming from other jurisdictions can be felt. For example, some features of the civil law system (such as extended factfinding without a concentrated time for a trial and the reliance on a judge to supervise the gathering of information) are beginning to be incorporated in the common law system (through exchanges in discovery and the increasingly managerial stance of judges).

Return then to the larger question of which the federal system has often been used as an illustration. What institutions ought to be responsible for determining the rules by which decisions are made in adjudicatory systems? If rulemaking is understood to be primarily a problem of craft and expertise, then committing it to specialized bodies has appeal. If rulemaking is also seen as entailing significant political decisions about the quantum of process requisite to rendering judgments enforced by government and the appropriate allocation of power among private parties and government officials, then specialized bodies may not provide adequate legitimacy as they give answers to societal questions through their rule drafting. And when rules aspire to cross national boundaries, what are the sources of their legitimacy?

The problem of making rules about process is, in turn, emblematic of the themes that have laced this book. Procedural systems are embedded in and expressive of the political cultures that empower and shape them. I have mapped the expansion and contraction of procedural opportunities, and I have detailed the proliferation of juridical institutions and the pressures to revamp judicial forms—all in the hopes of inviting readers into the richness and complexity of debates about what constitutes fair and just process.

INDEX

References are to Pages.

ADDITIONAL READINGS

This book cuts across many legal categories. I hope that readers will use the list below as an invitation to read further and that, in turn, the books and articles will be resources that lead to yet other materials. In addition to the citations listed below, I commend publications of several institutions, such as the American Bar Research Foundation, the American Law Institute, the Bureau of Justice Statistics, the Federal Judicial Center, the Institute for Civil Justice at RAND, the National Center for State Courts, the State Justice Institute, the United Nations, and the World Bank, all of which do research on the justice system.

Abel, Richard L. *An American Hamburger Stand in St. Paul's Cathedral: Replacing Legal Aid with Conditional Fees in English Personal Injury Litigation*, 51 DePaul Law Review 253 (2001).

Abel, Richard L. *The Legal Profession in England and Wales*, Basil Blackwell, (1988).

Abel, Richard L., & Lewis, Philip S.C. *Lawyers in Society: An Overview* (U. Cal. 1995).

Alschuler, Albert W. & Deiss, Andrew G. *A Brief History of the Criminal Jury in the United States*, 61 U. Chi. L. Rev. 867 (1994).

American Bar Association, Model Rules of Professional Conduct (2002).

American Law Institute, ALI/Unidroit, Principles and Rules of Transnational Civil Procedure, Discussion Draft No. 3, April 2003.

Andrews, Neil. *Multi–Party Proceedings in England: Representative and Group Actions*, 11 Duke J. Comp. & Int'l L. 259 (2001).

Babcock, Barbara. *Voir Dire: Preserving "Its Wonderful Power,"* 27 Stan. L. Rev. 545 (1975).

Bahdi, Reem. *Globalization of Judgment: Transadjudication and the Five Faces of International Law in Domestic Courts*, 34 Geo. Wash. Int'l L. Rev. 555 (2002).

Baker, Lynn A., & Silver, Charles. *Civil Justice Fact and Fiction*, 80 Tex. L. Rev. 1537 (2002).

Ball, Milner S. *Constitution, Court, Indian Tribe*, 1987 Am. Found. Res. J. 1.

Bermat, Gordon. Jury Selection Procedures in the United States District Courts (Federal Judicial Center, 1982).

Bone, Robert G. *Statistical Adjudication: Rights, Justice, and Utility in a World of Procedural Scarcity*, 46 Vand. L. Rev. 565 (1993).

Bone, Robert G. *The Economics of Civil Procedure* (Foundation Press, 2003).

Bone, Robert G. *The Process of Making Process: Court Rulemaking, Democratic Legitimacy, and Procedural Efficacy*, 87 Geo. L. J. 887 (1999).

Bradley, Curtis A. *The Costs of International Human Rights Litigation*, 2 Chi. J. Int'l L. 457 (2001).

Braithwaite, John. Restorative Justice & Responsive Regulation (Oxford 2002).

Brazil, Wayne D.. & Smith, Jennifer. *Choice of Structures: Critical Values and Concerns Should Guide Format of Court ADR Programs*, 6 Disp. Resol. Mag. 8 (1999).

Brazil, Wayne D. *The Adversary Character of Civil Discovery: A Critique and Proposals for Change*, 31 Vand. L. Rev. 1295 (1978).

Brunet, Edward, & Craver, Charles B. Alternative Dispute Resolution: The Advocate's Perspective (1997).

153

Burbank, Stephen B. *The Rules Enabling Act of 1934*, 130 U. PA. L. REV. 1015 (1982).

Carrington, Paul. *Judicial Independence and Democratic Accountability in Highest State Courts*, 61 LAW & CONTEMP. PROB. 79 (1998).

Chase, Oscar. *American "Exceptionalism" and Comparative Procedure*, 50 AM. J. COMP. L. 277 (2002).

Chayes, Abram. *The Role of the Judge in Public Law Litigation*, 89 HARV. L. REV. 1281 (1976).

Clark, Charles E. *The Influence of Federal Procedural Reform*, 13 LAW & CONTEMP. PROBS. 144 (1948).

Clark, Charles E. *The Role of the Supreme Court in Federal Rule–Making*, 46 J. AM. JUDICATURE SOC'Y 250 (1963).

Clark, Charles E., & Moore, James Wm. *A New Federal Civil Procedure—I. The Background*, 44 YALE L.J. 387 (1935).

Clermont, Kevin M. *Jurisdictional Salvation and the Hague Treaty*, 85 CORNELL L. REV. 89 (1999).

Clermont, Kevin M., & Eisenberg, Theodore. *Litigation Realities*, 88 CORNELL L. REV. 119 (2002).

Coffee, John C., Jr. *Class Action Accountability: Reconciling Exit, Voice, and Loyalty in Representative Litigation*, 100 COLUM. L. REV. 370 (2000).

COOPER, LAURA J., NOLAN, DENNIS R., & BALES, RICHARD A. ADR IN THE WORKPLACE (2000).

Cooter, Robert D., & Rubinfeld, Daniel L. *An Economic Model of Legal Discovery*, 23 J. LEG. STUD. 435 (1994).

Cover, Robert M. *For James Wm. Moore: Some Reflections on a Reading of the Rules*, 84 YALE L.J. 718 (1975).

Cover, Robert M. *Justice Accused* (Yale University Press, 1975).

Cover, Robert M. *The Supreme Court, 1982 Term—Foreword, Nomos and Narrative*, 97 HARV. L. REV. 4 (1983).

Cover, Robert M. *Violence and the Word*, 95 YALE L.J. 1601 (1986).

Cover, Robert M. and Fiss, Owen M. *The Structure of Procedure* (Foundation Press, 1979).

Cover, Robert M. Fiss, Owen M. and Resnik, Judith. *Procedure* (Foundation Press, 1988).

Cull, The Hon. Lord. *Review of the Business of the Outer House of the Court of Session* (Scottish Courts Administration, Edinburgh, 1995).

Curtis, Dennis E. *Grieving Criminal Defense Lawyers*, 70 FORDHAM L. REV. 1615 (2002).

Damaska, Mirjan. *Evidence Law, Adrift* (Yale Press, 1997).

Damaska, Mirjan. *Presentation of Evidence and Factfinding Precision*, 123 U. PA. L. REV. 1083 (1975).

DAVIS, MARTHA. BRUTAL NEED: LAWYERS AND THE WELFARE RIGHTS MOVEMENT, 1960–1973 (1993).

De Frances, Carol & Litras, Marika F.X. *Civil Trial Cases and Verdicts in Large Counties*, 1996, Bureau of Justice Statistics, NCJ 173426 (Sept. 1999).

Djankov, Simeon; La Porta, Rafael; Lopez-de-Silanes, Florencio; Shleifer, Andrei. *Courts: The Lex Mundi Project*, Harv. Inst. Economic Research (HIER), Discussion Paper No. 1951, March 2002.

Eisenberg, Theodore & Yeazell, Stephen C. *The Ordinary and the Extraordinary in Institutional Litigation*, 93 HARV. L. REV. 465 (1980).

Eskridge, William N., Jr. *Textualism, The Unknown Ideal?*, 96 MICH. L. REV. 1509 (1998).

Essays on Transnational and Comparative Civil Procedure (eds. Federico Carpi & Michele Angelo Lupoi) (G. Giappichelli Editore, 2001).

Ewick, Patricia & Silbey, Susan S. *The Common Place of Law* (U. Chicago Press, 1998).

Fallon, Richard, H., Meltzer, Daniel J., and Shapiro, David L., Hart and Wechsler's *The Federal Courts and the Federal System* (Foundation Press, 5th ed. 2003).

Farina, Cynthia. *On Misusing "Revolution" and "Reform": Procedural Due Process and the New Welfare Act*, 50 ADMIN. L. REV. 591 (1998).

FEDERAL JUDICIAL CENTER, MANUAL FOR COMPLEX LITIGATION (1995) (2004).

Felstiner, William L.F., *Influences of Social Organization on Dispute Processing*, 9 LAW & SOCIETY REV. 63 (1974).

Field, Martha. *Source of Law: The Scope of Federal Common Law*, 99 HARV. L. REV. 881 (1986).

Fisch, Jill E. *Lawyers on the Auction Block: Evaluating the Selection of Class Counsel by Auction*, 102 COLUM. L. REV. 650 (2002).

Fisher, George. *Plea Bargaining's Triumph*, 109 YALE L.J. 857 (2000).

Fiss, Owen M. *Against Settlement*, 93 YALE L.J. 1073 (1984).

Fiss, Owen M. *The Allure of Individualism*, 78 IOWA L. REV. 981 (1993).

Fiss, Owen M. *The Forms of Justice*, 93 HARV. L. REV. 1 (1979).

Fiss, Owen M. *The Political Theory of the Class Action*, 53 WASH. & LEE L. REV. 21 (1996).

Fiss, Owen M. *The Social and Political Foundations of Adjudication*, 6 LAW & HUM. BEHAV. 121 (1982).

Fiss, Owen M. and Resnik, Judith. *Adjudication and Its Alternatives: An Introduction to Procedure* (Foundation Press, 2003).

Fletcher, William. *The Structure of Standing*, 98 YALE L.J. 221 (1988).

Fouchard Gaillard, *Goldman on International Commercial Arbitration* (eds. Emmanuel Gaillard & John Savage) Kluwer Law International (1999).

Friedenthal, Jack H. *Secrecy in Civil Litigation: Discovery and Party Agreements*, 9 J.L. & POL'Y 67 (2000).

Fuller, Lon. *The Forms and Limits of Adjudication*, 92 HARV. L. REV. 353 (1978).

Galanter, Marc. *Jury Shadows: Reflections on the Civil Jury and the "Litigation Explosion"* in THE AMERICAN CIVIL JURY: FINAL REPORT OF THE 1986 CHIEF JUSTICE EARL WARREN CONFERENCE ON ADVOCACY IN THE UNITED STATES 15 (1987).

Galanter, Marc. *"Why the 'Haves' Come Out Ahead: Speculations on the Limits of Legal Change."* 9 LAW & SOCIETY REVIEW 95, 1972.

Galligan, D.J. *Due Process and Fair Procedures: A Study of Administrative Procedures* (Oxford, 1996).

Garth, Bryant G. *From Civil Litigation to Private Justice: Legal Practice at War with the Profession and Its Values*, 59 BROOK. L. REV. 931 (1993).

Garth, Bryant G. *Two Worlds of Civil Discovery: From Studies to the Markets in Legal Services and Legal Reform*, 39 B.C. L. REV. 597 (1998).

Genn, Hazel. *Paths to Justice: What People Do and Think About Going to Law* (Oxford, 1999).

Glanfield, Laurie, and Wright, Ted. *Model Key Performance Indicators for New South Wales Courts* (Australia, Justice Research Center, 2000).

GLASPELL, SUSAN. A JURY OF HER PEERS (1917).

GOLDBERG, STEPHEN B., SANDER, FRANK E., & ROGERS, NANCY H. DISPUTE RESOLUTION: NEGOTIATION, MEDIATION, AND OTHER PROCESSES (1999).

Goldstein, Stephen. *The Utility of the Comparative Perspective in Understanding, Analyzing, and Reforming Procedural Law* (U. Oxford, Institute of European and Comparative Law, Oxford, 1999).

Gross, Samuel R. & Syverod, Kent D. *Don't Try: Civil Juries in a System Geared to Settlement*, 44 UCLA L. REV. 1 (1996).

Grundfest, Joseph A., & Perino, Michael A. *Joint Testimony, Ten Things We Know and Ten Things We Don't Know About the Private Securities Litigation Reform Act of 1995*, 1015 PLI/CORP. 1015 (1997).

Gulati, Mitu, & McCauliff, C.M.A. *On Not Making Law*, 61 LAW & CONTEMP. PROBS. 157 (1997).

Guthrie, Chris, Rachlinski, Jeffrey J., & Wistrich, Andrew J. *Inside the Judicial Mind*, 86 CORNELL L. REV. 777 (2001).

Hand, Learned. *Historical and Practical Considerations Regarding Expert Testimony*, 15 HARV. L. REV. 40 (1901).

HANS, VALERIE P., & VIDMAR, NEIL. JUDGING THE JURY (1986).

Hastie, Reid, & Viscusi, Kip W. *What Juries Can't Do Well: The Jury's Performance as a Risk Manager*, 40 ARIZ. L. REV. 901 (1998).

Hazard, Geoffrey C. *A General Theory of State–Court Jurisdiction*, 1965 SUP. CT. REV. 241.

Hazard, Geoffrey C., Jr. *Undemocratic Legislation*, 87 YALE L.J. 1284 (1978).

Heinz, John P. & Edward O. Laumann, *Chicago Lawyers: The Social Structure of the Bar* (rev. ed. 1994).

Hensler, Deborah R. *A Research Agenda: What We Need to Know About Court–Connected ADR*, 6 Disp. Resol. Mag. 15 (1999).

Hensler, Deborah R. *As Time Goes By: Asbestos Litigation after Anchem and Ortiz*, 80 Tex. L. Rev. 1899 (2002).

Hensler, Deborah R., Bonnie Dombrey-Moore, Beth Giddens, Jennifer Gross, Erik Moller & Nicholas M. Pace. *Class Actions Dilemmas: Pursuing Public Goals for Private Gain* (RAND, 2000).

Heydebrand, Wolf & Seron, Carroll. Rationalizing Justice: The Political Economy of Federal District Courts (New York State Press, 1990).

Hill, Alfred. *The Judicial Function in Choice of Law*, 85 Colum. L. Rev. 1585 (1985).

Hume Papers on Public Policy: The Reform of Civil Justice (Edinburgh University Press, 1997); Justice and Money (eds. Joelle Godard and David Guild, Edinburgh University Press, 1999).

Issacharoff, Samuel. *Class Action Conflicts*, 30 U.C. Davis L. Rev. 805 (1997).

Issacharoff, Samuel. *Governance and Legitimacy in the Law of Class Actions*, 1999 Sup. Ct. Rev. 377.

Issacharoff, Samuel. *When Substance Mandates Procedure: Martin v. Wilks and the Rights of Vested Incumbents in Civil Rights Consent Decrees*, 77 Cornell L. Rev. 189 (1992).

Judicial Independence in the EU Accession Process (Open Society Institute, 2001).

Justice, William Wayne. *The Origins of Ruiz v. Estelle*, 43 Stan L. Rev. 1 (1990).

Justices: Ce Qui a Change Dans La Justice Depuis 20 Ans (Dalloz, 1999).

Kaplow, Louis, & Shavell, Steven. *Fairness Versus Welfare*, 114 Harv. L. Rev. 961 (2001).

Kennedy, Randall. Race, Crime, and the Law (1977).

Kerber, Linda. No Constitutional Right to Be Ladies (1998).

Kerr, Norbert L., MacCoun, Robert J., and Kramer, Jeffrey P. *Bias in Judgment: Comparing Individuals and Groups*, 103 Psych. Rev. 687 (1996).

King, Nancy Jean. *Priceless Process: Nonnegotiable Features of Criminal Litigation*, 47 UCLA L. Rev. 113 (1999).

King, Nancy Jean. *The American Criminal Jury*, 62 Law & Contemp. Probs. 41 (1999).

Kirby, Michael, *Reform the Law: Essays on the Renewal of the Australian Legal System* (1983).

Klement, Alon. *Who Should Guard the Guardians? A New Approach for Monitoring Class Action Lawyers*, 21 Rev. of Litig. 25 (2002).

Langbein, John H. *The German Advantage in Civil Procedure*, 52 U. Chi. L. Rev. 823 (1985).

Laycock, Douglas. *Due Process of Law in Trilateral Disputes*, 78 Iowa L. Rev. 1011 (1993).

Lesnick, Howard. *The Federal Rule–Making Process: A Time for Reexamination*, 61 A.B.A. J. 579 (1975).

Levine, David I., Dorenberg, Donald L., and Nelken, Melissa L. *Civil Procedure Anthology* (Anderson, 1998).

Leubsdorf, John. *Ideals, Realities, and Lawyer Fees*, 4 Geo. J. Legal Ethics 581 (1997).

Leubsdorf, John. *The Structure of Judicial Opinions*, 86 Minn. L. Rev. 557 (2001).

Liebman, James S. *The Overproduction of Death*, 100 Colum L. Rev. 2030 (2000).

Lind, E. Allan, MacCoun, Robert J., Ebener, Patricia A., Felstiner, William L. F., Hensler, Deborah R., Resnik, Judith, and Tyler, Tom R. *In the Eye of the Beholder: Tort Litigants' Perceptions of Trial, Arbitration, Bi–Lateral Negotiations, and Judicial Settlement*, 24 Law & Society Review 953 (1990), also published by Rand (Institute for Civil Justice, 1989).

Lind, E. Allan and Tom R. Tyler. *The Social Psychology of Procedural Justice* (Plenum Press, 1988).

Little, Rory K. *The Federal Death Penalty: History and Some Thoughts on the Department of Justice's Role*, 26 FORDHAM URB. L.J. 347 (1999).

LOWENFELD, ANDREAS F. INTERNATIONAL LITIGATION AND ARBITRATION (1993).

MacCoun, Robert J., Lind, E. Allen, & Tyler, Tom R. *Alternative Dispute Resolution in Trial and Appellate Courts, in* HANDBOOK OF PSYCHOLOGY AND LAW (D.K. Kagehiro & W.S. Laufer eds., 1992).

MACNEIL, IAN. AMERICAN ARBITRATION LAW: REFORMATION, NATIONALIZATION, INTERNATIONALIZATION (1992).

Marcus, Richard L. *Confronting the Future: Coping with Discovery of Electronic Material*, 64 LAW & CONTEMP. PROBS. 253 (2001).

Marcus, Richard L. *Discovery Containment Redux*, 39 B.C. L. REV. 747 (1998).

Marder, Nancy S. *Juries, Justice & Multiculturalism*, 75 S. CAL. L. REV. 707 (2002).

Marder, Nancy S. *The Interplay of Race and False Claims of Jury Nullification*, 32 U. MICH. J.L. REFORM 285 (1999).

Marder, Nancy S. *The Myth of the Nullifying Jury*, 93 NW. U. L. REV. 877 (1999).

Marshall, Enid, A. *Gill: The Law of Arbitration* (4th ed. Sweet & Maxwell, 2001).

Mashaw, Jerry L. *The Supreme Court's Due Process Calculus for Administrative Adjudication in Mathews v. Eldridge: Three Factors in Search of a Theory of Value*, 44 U. CHI. L. REV. 28 (1976).

Massaro, Toni M. *Peremptories or Peers?—Rethinking Sixth Amendment Doctrine, Images, and Procedures*, 64 N.C. L. REV. 501 (1986).

Menkel–Meadow, Carrie. *Do the "Haves" Come Out Ahead in Alternative Dispute Resolution Systems?: Repeat Players in ADR*, 15 OHIO ST. J. ON DISP. RES. 19 (1999).

Menkel–Meadow, Carrie. *Whose Dispute is It Anyway?: A Philosophical and Democratic Defense of Settlement (In Some Cases)*, 83 GEO. L.J. 2663 (1995).

Merkin, Robert, *An Arbitration Act of 1996: An Annotated Guide* (Lloyd's Commercial Law Library, 1996).

Michelman, Frank I. *The Supreme Court and Litigation Access Fees: The Right to Protect One's Rights*, 1973 DUKE L.J. 1153.

Miller, Arthur R. *The Pretrial Rush to Judgment: Are the "Litigation Explosion," "Liability Crisis," and Efficiency Cliches Eroding Our Day in Court and Jury Trial Commitments?*, 78 N.Y. U. L. REV. 982 (2003).

Miller, Arthur R., & Crump, David. *Jurisdiction and Choice of Law in Multistate Class Actions after Phillips Petroleum Co. v. Shutts*, 96 YALE L.J. 1 (1986).

Miller, Charles A. *The Forest of Due Process Law: The American Constitutional Tradition, in* 18 NOMOS 3 (J. Pennock and J. Chapman eds., 1977).

Miller, Geoffrey P., & Singer, Lori S. *Nonpecuniary Class Action Settlements*, 60 LAW & CONTEMP. PROBS. 97 (1997).

Moley, Raymond. *The Vanishing Jury*, 2 S. CAL. L. REV. 97 (1928).

Motomura, Hiroshi. *Arbitration and Collateral Estoppel: Using Preclusion to Shape Procedural Choices*, 63 TUL. L. REV. 29 (1988).

Mullenix, Linda S. *The Counter–Revolution in Procedural Justice*, 77 MINN. L. REV. 375 (1992).

Mustill, Michael J. & Boyd, Stewart C. *Commercial Arbitration, 2001 Companion Volume to the Second Edition* (Buttersworth, 2001).

Ninth Circuit Gender Bias Task Force, *The Effects of Gender: The Final Report of the Ninth Circuit Gender Bias Task Force*, republished, 67 SOUTHERN CALIFORNIA LAW REVIEW 727 (1994).

NOONAN, JOHN T., JR. NARROWING THE NATION'S POWER: THE SUPREME COURT SIDES WITH THE STATES (2002).

Nordh, Robert. *Group Actions in Sweden: Reflections on the Purpose of Civil Litigation, The Need for Reforms, and a Forthcoming Proposal*, 11 DUKE J. COMP. & INT'L L. 381 (2001).

Oakley, John B. *Integrating Supplemental Jurisdiction and Diversity Jurisdiction: A Progress Report on the Work of the American Law Institute*, 74 IND. L. REV. 25 (1998).

Oakley, John B., & Coon, Arthur. *The Federal Rules in State Courts: A Survey of State Court Systems of Civil Procedure*, 61 Wash. L. Rev. 1367 (1986).

Palmer, Michael & Roberts, Simon. *Dispute Processes: ADR and the Primary Forms of Decision Making* (Butterworths, 1998).

Park, William W. *Duty and Discretion in International Arbitration*, 93 Am. J. Int'l L. 804 (1999).

Parker, Christine. *Just Lawyers: Regulation and Access to Justice* (Oxford, 1999).

Parry, John T. *The Lost History of International Extradition Litigation*, 43 Va. J. Int'l L. 93 (2002).

Pennington, Nancy, & Hastie, Reid. *A Cognitive Theory of Juror Decision Making: The Story Model*, 13 Cardozo L. Rev. 519 (1991).

Perdue, Wendy Collins. *Sin, Scandal, and Substantive Due Process: Personal Jurisdiction and Pennoyer Reconsidered*, 62 Wash. L. Rev. 479 (1987).

Peters, Philip G., Jr. *Hindsight Bias and Tort Liability: Avoiding Premature Conclusions*, 31 Ariz. St. L. J. 1277 (2000).

Petersmann, Ernst–Ulrich. *Dispute Settlement in International Economic Law—Lessons for Strengthening International Dispute Settlement in Non–Economic Areas*, Journal of International Economic Law 189–248 (Oxford Press, 1999).

Peterson, Mark. *Civil Juries in the 1980s: Trends in Jury Trials and Verdicts in California and Cook County, Illinois* (RAND Institute for Civil Justice, 1987).

Purcell, Edward A., Jr. Brandeis and the Progressive Constitution: Erie, the Judicial Power, and the Politics of the Federal Courts in the Twentieth-Century America (Yale Press, 2000).

Purcell, Edward A., Jr. Litigation and Inequality: Federal Diversity Jurisdiction in Industrial America, 1870–1958 (1992).

Rabin, Robert L. *The Tobacco Litigation: A Tentative Assessment*, 51 DePaul L. Rev. 331 (2002).

Rachlinski, Jeffrey J. *Gains, Losses, and the Psychology of Litigation*, 70 S. Cal. L. Rev. 113 (1996).

Rauma, David, & Stienstra, Donna. *The Civil Justice Reform Act Expense and Delay Reduction Plans: A Sourcebook* (Federal Judicial Center, 1995).

Reform of Civil Procedure: Essays on Access to Justice (eds. A.A.S. Zuckerman & Ross Cranston, Oxford, 1995).

Reich, Charles. *The New Property*, 73 Yale L.J. 733 (1964).

Report of the Special Rapporteur on the Independence of Judges and Lawyers (United Nations 2001).

Resnik, Judith. *Changing Practices, Changing Rules: Judicial and Congressional Rulemaking on Civil Juries, Civil Justice, and Civil Judging*, 49 Ala. L. Rev. 133 (1997).

Resnik, Judith. *Dependent Sovereigns: Indian Tribes, States, and the Federal Courts*, 56 U. Chi. L. Rev. 671 (1989).

Resnik, Judith. *Failing Faith: Adjudicatory Procedure in Decline*, 53 U. Chi. L. Rev. 494 (1986).

Resnik, Judith. *Finding the Factfinders, in* The Verdict: Assessing the Civil Jury System 500 (Robert Litan ed., 1993).

Resnik, Judith. *From "Cases" to "Litigation,"* 54 Law & Contemp. Probs. 5 (Summer 1991).

Resnik, Judith. *Judging Consent*, 1987 U. Chi. Legal Forum 43.

Resnik, Judith. *Litigating and Settling Class Actions: The Prerequisites of Entry and Exit*, 30 U.C. Davis L. Rev. 835, 881 (1997).

Resnik, Judith. *Managerial Judges*, 96 Harv. L. Rev. 374 (1982).

Resnik, Judith. *Many Doors? Closing Doors? Alternative Dispute Resolution and Adjudication*, 10 Ohio St. J. on Disp. Resol. 211 (1995).

Resnik, Judith. *Money Matters: Judicial Market Interventions Creating Subsidies and Awarding Fees and Costs in Individual and Aggregate Litigation*, 148 U. Pa. L. Rev. 2119 (2000).

Resnik, Judith. *The Programmatic Judiciary: Lobbying, Judging, and Invalidating the Violence Against Women Act*, 74 S. Cal. L. Rev. 269 (2000).

Resnik, Judith. *Trial as Error, Jurisdiction as Injury: Transforming the Meaning of Article III*, 113 Harv. L. Rev. 924 (2000).

Resnik, Judith. *Whose Judgment? Vacating Judgments, Preferences for Settlement, and the Role of Adjudication at the Close of the Twentieth Century*, 41 UCLA L. REV. 1471 (1994).

Review of the Court of Appeal (Civil Division); Report to the Lord Chancellor (September, 1997) (Bowman Report).

Richardson, Genevra & Genn, Hazel. *Administrative Law and Government Action* (Oxford Press, 1994).

Robel, Lauren. *The Practice of Precedent*, 35 IND. L. REV. 299 (2002).

Roth, Kenneth. *The Court the U.S. Doesn't Want*, N.Y. REV. BOOKS (Nov. 1, 1998).

Rowe, Thomas D., Jr. *A Square Peg in a Round Hole? The 2000 Limitations on the Scope of Federal Civil Discovery*, 69 TENN. L. REV. 13 (2001).

Rowe, Thomas D., Jr., & Sibley, Kenneth. *Beyond Diversity: Federal Multiparty, Multiforum Jurisdiction*, 135 U. PA. L. REV. 7 (1986).

Rubenstein, William B. *The Concept of Equality in Civil Procedure*, 23 CARDOZO L. REV. 1865 (2002).

Rubino–Sammarano, *International Arbitration: Law and Practice* (2d ed. 2001, Kluwer Law Int'l).

Russell, Peter H. & O'Brien, David M. *Judicial Independence in the Age of Democracy: Critical Perspectives from Around the World* (U. Virginia Press, 2001).

Saks, Michael J., & Kidd, Robert F. *Human Information Processing and Adjudication: Trial by Heuristics*, 15 LAW & SOC'Y 123 (1980–81).

Schuck, Peter. *Agent Orange on Trial* (Harvard Press, 1987).

Shapiro, David L. *The Class Action: The Class As Party and Client*, 73 NOTRE DAME L. REV. 913 (1998).

Shavell, Steven. *Suit, Settlement, and Trial: A Theoretical Analysis under Alternative Methods for the Allocation of Legal Costs*, 11 JOURNAL LEGAL STUDIES 55 (1982).

Shepherd, George B. *Fierce Compromise: The Administrative Procedure Act Emerges From New Deal Politics*, 90 NW. U. L. REV. 1557 (1996).

Silberman, Linda J. *Judicial Jurisdiction in the Conflict of Laws Course: Adding a Comparative Dimension*, 1995 VAND. J. TRANSNAT'L L. 389 (1995).

Silberman, Linda J., & Lowenfeld, Andreas F. *A Different Challenge for the ALI: Herein of Foreign Country Judgments, An International Treaty, and An American Statute*, 75 IND. L.J. 635 (2000).

Silver, Charles. *Does Civil Justice Cost Too Much?*, 80 TEX. L. REV. 2073 (2002).

Slaughter, Anne–Marie. *A Typology of Transnational Communication*, 29 U. RICH. L. REV. 99 (1994).

Slaughter, Ann–Marie. *Judicial Globalization*, 40 VA. J. INTER'L L. 1103 (2002).

Slaughter, Ann–Marie. *The Global Community of Courts*, 44 HARV. INT'L L. J. 191 (2003).

Steinman, Joan. *The Effects of Case Consolidation on the Procedural Rights of Litigants: What They Are, What They Might Be, Part II: Non–Jurisdictional Matters*, 42 UCLA L. REV. 967 (1995).

Stemple, Jeffrey W. *Ulysses Tied to the Generic Whipping Post: The Continuing Odyssey of Discovery "Reform,"* 64 LAW & CONTEMP. PROBS. 197 (2001).

STERN, ROBERT L., GRESSMAN, EUGENE, SHAPIRO, STEPHEN M., & GELLER, KENNETH S. SUPREME COURT PRACTICE (8th ed. 2002).

Sternlight, Jean R. *As Mandatory Binding Arbitration Meets the Class Action, Will the Class Action Survive?*, 42 WM. & MARY L. REV. 1 (2000).

Sternlight, Jean R. *Forum Shopping for Arbitration Decisions: Federal Courts' Use of Antisuit Injunctions Against State Courts*, 147 U. PA. L. REV. 147 (1998).

Stith, Kate and Cabranes, Jose A. *Fear of Judging: Sentencing Guidelines in the Federal Courts* (U Chi. Press, 1998.)

Stone, Christopher D. *Should Trees Have Standing?—Toward Legal Rights for Natural Objects*, 45 S. CAL. L. REV. 450 (1972).

Stone, Katherine V.W. *Arbitration Law* (Foundation, 2003).

STONE, KATHERINE VAN WEZEL. PRIVATE JUSTICE: THE LAW OF ALTERNATIVE DISPUTE RESOLUTION (2000).

Stone, Katherine Van Wezel. *Rustic Justice: Community and Coercion Under the Federal Arbitration Act*, 77 N.C. L. REV. 931 (1999).

Struve, Catherine T. *The Paradox of Delegation: Interpreting the Federal*

Rules of Civil Procedure, 150 U. PA. L. REV. 1099 (2002).

Sturm, Susan. *Resolving the Judicial Dilemma: Strategies of Judicial Intervention in Prisons*, 138 U. PA. L. REV. 807 (1990).

Subrin, Stephen N. *How Equity Conquered Common Law: The Federal Rules of Civil Procedure in Historical Perspective*, 135 U. PA. L. REV. 909 (1987).

Sunstein, Cass. *What's Standing After Lujan? Of Citizen Suits, "Injuries," and Article III*, 91 MICH. L. REV. 163 (1992).

Symposium: *American Bar Association Report on Perceptions of the U.S. Justice System*, 62 ALB. L. REV. 1307 (1999).

Symposium on Mediation, 2002 J. DISP. RES. 83–129.

Symposium on Multidistrict Litigation and Aggregation Alternatives, 31 SETON HALL L. REV. 877 (2001).

Symposium: *Research on Juries*, 11 JUST. SYS. J. 1 (1986).

Symposium: *The American Jury*, 43 LAW & CONTEMP. PROBS. 1 (1980).

Symposium: *The Common Law Jury*, 62 LAW & CONTEMP. PROBS. 1 (1999).

Symposium: *The Inevitability of the Eclectic: Liberating ADR from Ideology*, 2000 J. DISP. RES. 247.

Taruffo, Michele. *Some Remarks on Group Litigation in Comparative Perspective*, 11 DUKE J. COMP. & INT'L L. 405 (2001).

Thayer, James B. *The Jury and Its Development*, 5 HARV. L. REV. 249 (1892).

The Future of Legal Services: The Arthur Liman Colloquium Papers, 17 YALE L. & POL'Y REV. 287 (1998).

The Transformation of Legal Aid: Comparative and Historical Studies (ed. Francis Regan, Alan Paterson, Tamara Goriely & Don Fleming) (Oxford Press, 1999).

Thibaut, John, & Walker, Laurens. *A Theory of Procedure*, 66 CAL. L. REV. 541 (1978).

Thornburg, Elizabeth G. *Going Private: Technology, Due Process, and Internet Dispute Resolution*, 34 U.C. DAVIS L. REV. 151 (2000).

Tribe, Laurence. *Trial by Mathematics: Precision and Ritual in the Legal Process*, 84 HARV. L. REV. 1329 (1971).

Trubek, David M., Austin Sarat, William F. Felstiner, Herbert M. Kritzer, & Joel B. Grossman. "The Costs of Ordinary Litigation." 31 *UCLA Law Review* 72 (1983).

Twitchell, Mary. *Why We Keep Doing Business with Doing–Business Jurisdiction*, 2001 U. CHI. LEG. FORUM 171.

TYLER, TOM R., BOECKMANN, ROBERT J., SMITH, HEATHER J., AND HUO, YUEN, J. SOCIAL JUSTICE IN A DIVERSE SOCIETY (1997).

Van Schaack, Beth. *In Defense of Civil Redress: The Domestic Enforcement of Human Rights Norms in the Context of the Proposed Hague Judgments Convention*, 42 HARV. INT'L L.J. 141 (2001).

Verkuil, Paul. *Reflections Upon the Federal Administrative Judiciary*, 39 UCLA L. REV. 1341 (1992).

VINING, JOSEPH. LEGAL IDENTITY (1978).

Von Mehrer, Arthur T., & Trautman, Donald T. *Jurisdiction to Adjudicate: A Suggested Analysis*, 79 HARV. L. REV. 1121 (1966).

Wald, Patricia M. *Summary Judgment at Sixty*, 76 TEX. L. REV. 1897 (1998).

Waldman, Ellen A. *Identifying the Role of Social Norms in Mediation: A Multiple Model Approach*, 48 HAST. L. REV. 703 (1997).

Ware, Stephen J. *Default Rules from Mandatory Rules: Privatizing Law Through Arbitration*, 83 MINN. L. REV. 703 (1999).

WEINSTEIN, JACK B. REFORM OF COURT RULE-MAKING PROCEDURES (1977).

Weisbrod, Carol. *Images of the Woman Juror*, 9 HARV. WOMEN'S L.J. 59 (1986).

White, Lucie E. *Subordination, Rhetorical Survival Skills, and Sunday Shoes: Notes on the Hearing of Mrs. G*, 38 BUFF. L. REV. 1 (1990).

White, Welsh S. *Defendants Who Elect Execution*, 48 U. PITT. L. REV. 853 (1987).

WILKINSON, CHARLES. AMERICAN INDIANS, TIME, AND THE LAW (1987).

Willging, Thomas, Shepard, John, Stienstra, Donna and Miletich, Dean.

Discovery and Disclosure Practice, and Proposals for Change, (Federal Judicial Center, 1997).

Winter, Stephen. *The Metaphor of Standing and the Problem of Self–Governance*, 40 STAN. L. REV. 1371 (1988).

Wissler, Roselle L. *Court–Connected Mediation in General Civil Cases: What We Know from Empirical Research*, 17 OHIO ST. J. ON DISP. RESOL. 641 (2002).

Woolf, Harry. *Access to Justice—Final Report* (1996) [Woolf Report].

Yeazell, Stephen C. *Judging Rules, Ruling Judges*, 61 LAW & CONTEMP. PROBS. 229 (1998).

Yeazell, Stephen C. *Re–Financing Civil Litigation*, 51 DEPAUL L. REV. 183 (2001).

Yeazell, Stephen C. *The Misunderstood Consequences of Modern Civil Process*, 1994 WIS. L. REV. 631.

Zander, Michael, *The State of Justice* (London, 2000).

Zeisel, Hans, & Diamond, Shari S. *"Convincing Empirical Evidence" on the Six Member Jury*, 41 U. CHI. L. REV. 281 (1974).

Zeisel, Hans, & Diamond, Shari S. *The Jury Selection in the Mitchell–Stans Conspiracy Trial*, 1976 AM. B. FOUND. RES. J. 151.

Zuckerman, Adrian A.S. *Civil Justice in Crisis* (Oxford Press, 1999).

*

TABLE OF CASES

References are to Pages.

ACKNOWLEDGMENTS

This book grows out of many years of collaboration with Robert Cover and Owen Fiss. My thanks to them and to many other scholars, friends, and students in and of law, with whom I have had the pleasure of working. Thanks are also due to Jennifer Brown, Harold Koh, Nancy Marder, Kate Stith, Charles Weisselberg, Elizabeth Brundige, Lane Dilg, Jasmine Elwick, Alison MacKenzie, Sara Sternberg, Elizabeth Wright, Marilyn Cassella, Gene Coakley, and especially to Denny Curtis, Deborah Hensler, and Vicki Jackson.

†